LIVING THROUGH
THE PLAINS INDIAN WARS
1864–1890

Andrew Langley

Heinemann
LIBRARY

Chicago, Illinois

www.capstonepub.com
Visit our website to find out more information about Heinemann-Raintree books.

To order:
☎ Phone 888-454-2279
🖳 Visit www.capstonepub.com
to browse our catalog and order online.

©2012 Heinemann Library
an imprint of Capstone Global Library, LLC
Chicago, Illinois

Edited by Andrew Farrow and Megan Cotugno
Designed by Steve Mead
Original illustrations © Capstone Global Library Ltd
Picture research by Ruth Blair
Production by Eirian Griffiths
Originated by Capstone Global Library Ltd
Printed and bound in the United States of America, North Mankato, MN
15 14 13 12
10 9 8 7 6 5 4 3 2

Library of Congress Cataloging-in-Publication Data
Langley, Andrew, 1949-
   The Plains Indian wars 1864-1890 / Andrew Langley.
      p. cm.—(Living through. . .)
   Includes bibliographical references and index.
   ISBN 978-1-4329-5999-9 (hb)—ISBN 978-1-4329-6008-7 (pb) 1. Indians of North America—Wars—1866-1895. 2. Indians of North America—Wars—Great Plains. 3. Indians of North America—Great Plains—History—19th century—Chronology. I. Title.
   E83.866.L36 2012
   978.004'97—dc22   2011015925

052012
006707RP

Acknowledgments
The author and publishers are grateful to the following for permission to reproduce copyright material: ©Corbis: pp. 12, 17 (Bettmann), 29 (© Bettmann), 39 (© Layne Kennedy), 41, 43 (© Bettmann), 44, 54, 56, 59 (© Bettmann), 61, 63 (© Bettmann); ©Getty Images: pp. 31 (MPI), 32, (MPI), 34 (American Stock), 36 (Abraham Bogardus/George Eastman House), 51 (Kean Collection), 53 (MPI), 65 (Transcendental Graphics); ©Library of Congress: pp. 8 (Edward S. Curtis), 15, 18 (Jenks, Daniel A.), 22, 24, 49 (Remington, Frederic, 1861-1909); ©Photolibrary: p. 47 (Sergio Pitamitz/Robert Harding Travel).

Cover image of Sitting Bear reproduced with permission from © Corbis (© Stapleton Collection).

We would like to thank Strother Roberts for his invaluable help in the preparation of this book.

CONTENTS

Some words are printed in bold, **like this**. You can find out what they mean by looking in the glossary.

PEOPLES OF THE PLAINS

The Plains Indian Wars were some of the saddest conflicts ever fought in North America. They led to the tragic destruction of a unique way of life. One historian has written that American Indians "have gone down many paths to defeat, along many ways filled with pain and heartbreak, but none so much as this long, last trail."[1]

A DOOMED CIVILIZATION

The Plains Wars were fought during the second half of the 19th century. On one side were American Indian peoples such as the Sioux, who had lived and hunted on the area known as the Great Plains (see below) for many years. These peoples were the Plains Indians. On the other side were white people from the eastern United States, who wanted to travel through or settle on the Plains.

The conflict was not like most other wars. There were very few big battles, and the forces on each side were usually small. Most fighting took place in limited areas, generally between a single group of Plains Indians and local white troops. Sometimes several groups fought together against the invaders. But the Plains Indians had no chance of winning the war. There were simply too many white people, and these white Americans had better weapons.

THE GREAT PLAINS

The Great Plains cover a massive part of central North America. They stretch from Texas in the south almost to the Arctic Ocean in the north. Until the 1800s, the Plains were wide-open grasslands, with no farms or roads. There were few trees, but a huge amount of wildlife thrived there. Antelope, elk, rabbits, wolves, and **prairie chickens** lived there, along with enormous herds of buffalo (another name for bison).

Groups of American Indians lived on the Great Plains. Many of these were **nomads**, moving about as they hunted buffalo and

CANADA

Washington Blackfoot Sarcee Cree
                Gros Assiniboine
        Flathead Ventre   Hidatsa Minnesota
    Nez Perce Montana Crow   Mandan Sioux
Oregon   Idaho   Arikara
                        S Dakota   Wisconsin   New York   Maine
        S h o s h o n e Cheyenne o   Michigan
            Wyoming   u   x
                    Ponca Iowa   Pennsylvania New Jersey
                Nebraska Omaha Iowa   Washington DC Delaware
Nevada   Pawnee Oto   Indiana Ohio
        Utah   Arapaho   Illinois   Virginia
California   Ute Colorado   W Virginia
                        Kansas Missouri   Kentucky   N Carolina
                Kansas
                        Osage   Tennessee
        Apache   Kiowa   S Carolina
    Arizona   Oklahoma Arkansas   Georgia
        New Mexico   Cherokee   Alabama
                                                    Atlantic Ocean
            Comanche Wichita   Mississippi
                    Texas   Louisiana
                    Tonkawa   Florida

MEXICO

Pacific Ocean   0   400 miles
                            0   500 km

△ This map shows where the American Indian tribes of the
Great Plains lived in relation to modern states.

other animals. European explorers of the early 1800s reported that
the Plains were useless for settlers. A soldier, Major Stephen Long,
wrote in 1820 that the area was "unfit for cultivation [growing],
and of course uninhabitable [not capable of being lived on] by
a people depending on agriculture." He renamed it "The Great
American Desert."[2]

THE PLAINS INDIANS

In 1800 there were about 130,000 American Indians on the vast
expanse of the Great Plains.[3] They belonged to over 30 major groups
of people. The biggest group was the Sioux, or Dakota, **nation**, which
was made up of several different **tribes**. Other large groups included
the Blackfeet, Comanches, Cheyennes, and Pawnees. These tribes were
often at war with each other over territory or other disagreements.

...OUX VILLAGE

...eoples of the Plains lived a very free lifestyle. They did not stay ... in one place, but rather followed the enormous herds of buffalo across the **prairies**. They hunted these giant animals on horseback to get meat, **hides**, and other important materials. Each Indian **band**, ranging from a dozen people to more than 100, lived together in a village.

HOME ON THE PLAINS

Instead of permanent houses, the Sioux had large tents called tipis. These were tall and cone-shaped and covered with buffalo hides. They could be built or taken down very quickly when the band moved to another area. This was the job of the women, who were seen as the owners of the tipis.[4]

Parts of a tipi

Tipis had several basic parts:

- *Poles:* A big tipi was made up of as many as 20 wooden poles, and it stood over 20 feet (6 meters) high.[5] There were few trees on the Plains, so the Plains Indians often had to make long journeys to find their poles.

- *Coverings:* The outside of a tipi was covered with buffalo skins, with a second layer of skins inside the tipi, up to head height. These kept out the bitter winter winds.

- *Pegs:* The bottom of the tipi's covering was fixed to the ground with wooden pegs or with heavy rocks.

- *Smoke vent:* Smoke from the fire went out through a vent (gap) at the top of the tipi. There were flaps that could be closed to keep out the rain.

- *Doorway:* A tipi's doorway was an opening in the cover, which was protected by a hide curtain, with short poles fixed at the top and bottom. It usually faced east, where the sun rose.[6]

Inside each tipi was a small fire for cooking and heating. In hot weather, the lower part of the skin covering could be unpinned and propped up to let in cool air. But a tipi was also very cozy in winter. One Sioux man wrote: "On nights when there was a cold, sleeting rain, it was very pleasant to lie in bed and listen to the storm beating on the sides of the tipi."[7]

There were no chairs or tables—or even beds—in the tipi. The floor was covered with rugs or skins. Plains Indian men sat cross-legged on the floor, while the women sat on their heels or with their legs to one side. They leaned against backrests made of willow-twig frames tied together with cords. People sometimes made beds from these backrests, but most people slept on the floor wrapped in a buffalo skin.

Eyewitness

Flying Hawk (1852–1931) was a chief of the Oglala people, part of the Sioux nation. He lived on the Plains for the early part of his life. He said:

The tipi is much better to live in; always clean, warm in winter, cool in summer, easy to move. The white man builds big house, cost much money, like big cage, shut out sun; can never move; always sick. Indians and animals know better how to live than white man; nobody can be in good health if he does not have all the time fresh air, sunshine and good water.[8]

HUNTERS WITH HORSES

The Plains Indians had once lived a different lifestyle. For many centuries their only way of traveling on land was to walk. The only animals they kept were dogs, which they used to haul their belongings on a travois, a simple kind of sled with a platform. Hunting the big, heavy herds of buffalo was very difficult, because the Indians had to follow and stalk them on foot.

Then, from about 1500, the Spanish arrived in Central America. They brought with them from Europe a new kind of animal—the horse. In 1680 American Indians in New Mexico rebelled against the Spanish invaders and seized large herds of horses.[9] Many of these horses found their way to the tribes on the Plains. Now the Plains Indians could hunt on horseback and use horses to carry heavy loads. Soon they also obtained guns from the European settlers.

Three Sioux chiefs sit on horseback. Horses were used by the Plains Indians for hunting and carrying heavy loads.

RUNNING OUT OF ROOM

The arrival of the horse and the gun allowed the Plains Indians to develop a new way of life. Hunting became much easier. They could kill enough buffalo and other **game** animals to live off of throughout the year. They could wander where they liked, in search of food, water, and suitable places to camp. Each tribe had its own traditional hunting grounds.

This freedom did not last long. During the same period, on the East Coast of the United States, European settlements were growing fast. They spilled onto the lands of the Eastern Indian peoples, causing bitterness and warfare. When the United States became an independent country in 1776, its government began making **treaties** with American Indians. In exchange for money and goods, many tribes agreed to give territory to the whites.

THE INDIAN REMOVAL ACT

But such trades did not solve the problem. By the early 1800s, there was not enough land for both the American Indians and the huge numbers of European settlers to live together in peace. So the U.S. government decided on a simple and brutal plan. Many European settlers viewed the American Indians as members of an **uncivilized** race that was in the way of natural human progress. They believed that American Indians had to be moved to another part of the country.

The Trail of Tears

The Cherokee people of Georgia made up one of the biggest groups of Eastern Indians. They fought against the forced move west—not with bloodshed, but rather in the courts. The U.S. Supreme Court recognized their right to stay in Georgia, but President Andrew Jackson overruled this. So in the harsh winter of 1838, U.S. soldiers marched the Cherokees on their long trek west. Men, women, and children were forced to walk for nearly 1,000 miles (1,600 kilometers). Most had only thin clothing and bare feet. At least 4,000 of the Cherokees died from disease, hunger, or cold during the journey. This was a quarter of their total population. They called this journey the "Trail of Tears."[10]

Where could they go? The answer was obvious: to the Great Plains. These were vast and empty spaces, and few white people wanted to live there. In 1830 the U.S. Congress passed a law called the Indian Removal Act. This forced many Eastern Indian peoples to leave their traditional homes and settle on land in present-day Oklahoma, west of the Mississippi River. The area became known as **Indian Territory**.

HEADING WEST

By 1840 the removal of American Indians to the Great Plains was almost complete. More than 90,000 native men, women, and children had been forced to move from the East to the grasslands west of the Mississippi River.[1] Here, in Indian Territory, they joined the Plains Indian tribes who had lived here for generations. There were at least 250,000 of these people.[2]

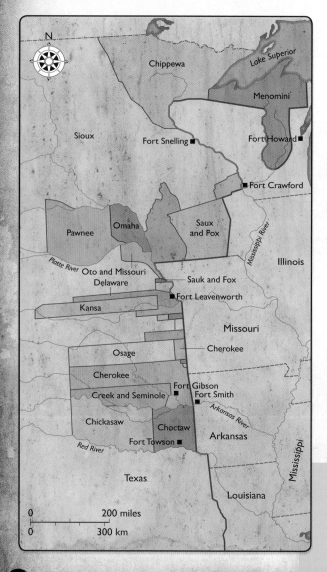

This map shows tribe locations in Indian Territory in the Great Plains (circa 1840).

WHERE WAS THE FRONTIER?

At this time, Indian Territory covered most of what is now the state of Oklahoma. Its boundary ran northward from the edge of present-day Texas to Lake Michigan. West of this lay the new homelands for many American Indian groups. Most white Americans believed this region to be worthless desert, where they would never want to settle.

This boundary, set in 1830, became known as the Permanent Indian **Frontier**.

The U.S. government promised that the American Indians would be able to stay beyond this "frontier," undisturbed forever. They could live independently as long as they remained peaceful. No white people would be allowed to settle on Indian land.

OUTSIDERS ON THE PLAINS

But these promises were quickly broken. White settlers and traders were soon pushing into the Indian Territory. Worse still, in 1848 gold was discovered in California. This meant that thousands of fortune hunters traveled across the Plains to get to the goldfields on the West Coast. The Permanent Indian Frontier had lasted just a few years.

Few settlers understood or cared about the American Indian way of life or **culture**. Many thought the native peoples were uncivilized beings who were barely human and deserved no respect. They were also horrified at many American Indian **rituals** and customs, which they viewed as violent. So large numbers of white **pioneers** and U.S. Army leaders believed the best way to deal with the Plains Indians was to **exterminate** them.

Another big problem for the Plains Indians was the upheaval caused by the arrival of the Eastern Indian tribes. The government had given them fixed areas of land to live on. But this often meant that the people who already lived there had to be moved as well, to make room for the newcomers. Not surprisingly, there was anger and violence among several neighboring American Indian groups.

Manifest Destiny

In 1845 a U.S. journalist named John O'Sullivan wrote that Americans had "the right of our **manifest destiny** to overspread and to possess the whole of the continent which Providence has given us."[3] He was writing about the U.S. government's plan to take over the territory of Texas, but his words described a widespread feeling among U.S. citizens. They believed they had a God-given right to expand westward across North America and seize land for their own use—even if others lived there already, such as the Plains Indians. The idea of Manifest Destiny was used to justify many decisions and actions by settlers and the U.S. government, no matter how many moral questions they raised.

LIFE IN A WAGON TRAIN

The journey to the West was a long one. Pioneers had to make their way over 2,000 miles (3,200 kilometers) of wilderness, including the Great Plains. Most people made the trip in two stages. The first stage was on a steamboat up the Missouri River to a port such as St. Joseph, Missouri, or Fort Kearney, Nebraska. From there, they had to travel across the land.

▽ Pioneers in covered wagons faced thirst, hunger, dust, and disease, as well as the threat of attack by Plains Indians.

THE PRAIRIE SCHOONER

Pioneer families traveled in simple wagons, which carried them and all their belongings. The wagons had wide wheels, so that they would not sink into the mud or dust. The wagon body was topped with hoops covered with canvas, which fluttered in the wind. For this reason, they were known as "prairie schooners." (A schooner is a type of sailing ship.) In these wagons, they seemed to sail over the rolling Plains.

Teams of four or six **oxen** hauled the wagons. Oxen walked slowly, but they were steadier than horses or mules. They were also strong enough to pull their loads through mud and shallow rivers. Where the water was deeper, the oxen had to swim across, with the prairie schooners floating behind them.[4]

A DAY ON THE TRAIL

At dawn, the men rounded up the oxen and harnessed them to the wagons. Each wagon train had a guide, who went ahead to decide on the route. The wagons followed slowly behind. There might be 50 wagons, stretching for nearly 1 mile (1.6 kilometers).

The oxen plodded along all day, except for a break at noon. By late afternoon they might have covered 12 to 20 miles (19 to 32 kilometers). The travelers parked the wagons in a circle at night. This was partly to form a **corral** to keep in oxen and other **livestock** and partly to protect against attacks by Plains Indians.[6]

Did you know?

An oxen driver walked along beside his team. This was easy, because the oxen moved very slowly. The driver carried a whip, which he cracked in the air to hurry the animals along. To make them turn left, he would shout "Woo-ah!" To turn right, he shouted "Gee!"[5]

The wagons carried a lot of food for the journey. It was mostly simple foods, such as flour, dried beans, bacon, lard, coffee, and salt. Meals at the end of the day did not vary much, unless someone had killed a buffalo or some other game. After dinner, the travelers sat around their cooking fires, telling stories, singing, or dancing to a fiddler.

Storms were frequent on the wide eastern Plains. Rain and hail blew so hard that the canvas covers on the wagons could be ripped off. The long wagon trains left deep ruts on the trail, which turned to deep mud in wet weather. Wheels became clogged with mud, forcing drivers to stop to clean them off.[7]

As the travelers went further west, the land became drier and sandier. There was no firewood, so they had to burn dried buffalo dung instead. Stinging dust swirled into their eyes and mouths. Water became scarce, and many of the springs they found were unfit to drink. Many pioneers became sick or died before they reached California.

THE FORT LARAMIE TREATY

Throughout the early 1850s, growing numbers of white settlers flooded across the Great Plains. Their wagons carved out clear roads, such as the Oregon Trail, which stretched from Missouri to present-day Oregon. Their livestock ate the grass near the trails. Their hunters cut down trees for firewood and shot hundreds of buffalo. Angry that their way of life was being threatened, Plains Indians increased their attacks on the white strangers.

The U.S. government looked for a way to prevent all-out war between the two sides. In 1851 agents from the Bureau of Indian Affairs (see box) called a meeting at Fort Laramie, near the Oregon Trail, in what is now eastern Wyoming. Over 10,000 Sioux, Cheyennes, and other American Indian peoples came. Most of them agreed to stop attacking the wagon trains and stay within the boundaries of their land. In exchange, the government paid them $50,000 a year.[8] This was shared among the different groups of American Indians.

The Bureau of Indian Affairs

In 1824 the U.S. government set up a new body for handling relations between the government and the many different American Indian peoples. Called the Bureau of Indian Affairs, it was under the control of the War Department. The bureau handled land treaties, the setting up of tribal schools, and trade between Indians and whites. It is still at work today.

MASSACRE AND REVENGE

The peace treaty lasted for nearly three years. Then, on August 19, 1854, a small incident sparked the first major violence on the Plains. A Sioux hunter, desperate for food, shot a stray cow belonging to a settler near Fort Laramie. The settler complained to the local U.S. Army commander. U.S. troops marched on the Sioux camp to demand payment for the cow. But there was an argument, and the soldiers opened fire with a cannon. The Sioux fought back, killing every soldier except one. This event is known as the Grattan **Massacre**, after the leader of the U.S. side, Lieutenant John Grattan.

The U.S. government took a terrible revenge for this massacre. On September 2 and 3, 1855, in present-day Garden County, Nebraska, a force of 600 U.S. soldiers attacked a small camp of Sioux, who had nothing to do with the killing or the cow. In the hail of bullets, 80 Sioux warriors were killed and 70 women and children were captured.[9] The remaining men were taken captive and imprisoned. This event was known as the Battle of Ash Hollow, or the Battle of Bluewater Creek.

LITTLE CROW'S UPRISING

By the 1860s, the flow of settlers had become a flood, and the U.S. Army built forts along the main trails to protect the settlers. Small towns had sprung up on the eastern Plains. The Sioux here had lost most of their hunting land to the whites, and they needed food and other materials to survive.

In 1862 the Sioux, led by their chief, Little Crow, decided that violence was better than starvation. They raided settlements and lone farms throughout southern Minnesota. Hundreds of whites were killed, and many thousands fled in terror. But before long an army of over 6,000 U.S. troops had swept through Minnesota. The uprising ended, and a white farmer shot Little Crow dead while the chief was picking berries.[10]

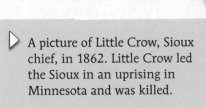

▷ A picture of Little Crow, Sioux chief, in 1862. Little Crow led the Sioux in an uprising in Minnesota and was killed.

THE PLAINS WARS

War on the Great Plains was now certain. There were simply too many white people crowding onto Indian Territory. U.S. government promises about a permanent and protected area for Indians were long forgotten. Plus, leaders in Washington, D.C., were not always able to control what happened far away on the Plains. Decisions were often made locally, and they reflected a common feeling of contempt for American Indians.

From the 1850s, the U.S. government had passed laws allowing white settlers and traders to take over parts of the Indian Territory. The different tribes were ordered to move onto areas called **reservations**, which had been set aside for them. These were often on land that was too poor for the Indians to grow food, and that were too small for them to hunt buffalo.

Not surprisingly, many Plains Indian groups refused to stay on their reservations. They wandered back to their old hunting grounds. In search of food, they sometimes stole cattle or horses from the white settlers, or they attacked wagon trains. Troops were kept busy trying to recover the stolen goods and take away the weapons of the Indians who posed a threat.

PUNISHING THE CHEYENNE

The southern Cheyennes had one of the worst reservations. Sand Creek, in present-day Colorado, was a sandy wasteland. About 200 warriors camped there, along with about 500 women and children. Their chief was Black Kettle (see box). The Cheyennes soon began raiding white settlements for food. Pioneers stopped using some of the nearby the trails. Many people left the region altogether.[1]

In November 1864, U.S. Colonel John Chivington led a force of 700 volunteer soldiers to the camp at Sand Creek. Chivington's order to his men was short and simple: "Kill and **scalp** all, big and little."[2] Scalping was the removal of the hair and skin on top of a person's head. It was very painful, but not necessarily fatal. American Indians used scalping to frighten their enemies, and to prove they that had conquered someone in battle.

Black Kettle c. 1812–1868

BORN: Probably born near the Black Hills of present-day South Dakota

ROLE: Leader of the Southern Cheyennes

In about 1854 Black Kettle became leader of the Southern Cheyennes. He quickly realized that the white men were more powerful than the Indians, and so he advised his people to make peace. When Chivington attacked the Sand Creek camp in 1864, Black Kettle still believed he could stop the violence. He raised a U.S. flag to show he was peaceful, but it had no effect. He survived the massacre, but he was killed in 1868 by troops led by George Custer at Washita River (see page 33).[3]

The 7th U.S. Cavalry (led by Lt. Col. Custer) attacks Black Kettle's camp near the Washita River in 1868. Black Kettle was killed during this battle.

SLAUGHTER AT SAND CREEK

At dawn, cannon and rifle fire blasted through the tipis. Then, Chivington and his men charged. The Cheyennes were caught by surprise and had few weapons with which to fight back. In the next few hours, the soldiers slaughtered any Indian they could see. At least 160 Cheyennes died, most of them women and children. Many were scalped and savagely cut open.[4]

WILLIAM BENT

William Bent was born in St. Louis, in present-day Missouri. His father was a wealthy judge, and William had an expensive education. But he soon became fascinated by the lives of American Indians. He learned to speak Sioux and use Indian sign language.

MARRIED INTO THE CHEYENNES

In 1829 Bent made a trip with his brother along the Santa Fe Trail, which connected Missouri to present-day New Mexico. He loved the frontier country and stayed there, making his living as a **fur trapper**. He also made his first contact with the Plains Indians, when he rescued two Cheyenne men who were being attacked by Comanches.

This marked the beginning of a long and close friendship with the Cheyennes of this band.

Bent lived with them for long periods, and he married Owl Woman, the daughter of a Cheyenne chief. The couple had five children. When Owl Woman died in 1847, Bent married her sister, named Yellow Woman.

The world of the half-breed

Anyone born of mixed white and American Indian parents was called a half-breed. These people often had difficult lives, despised by both races. William Bent's children were all half-breeds. Three of them eventually abandoned the world of the white people and went to live with the Cheyenne.

PEACEMAKER

The marriages helped Bent to become one of the few white men to be trusted by the Cheyennes. They even gave him a nickname, "Little White Man."[5] Black Kettle and other leaders often went to him for help and advice, and he became an important middleman in dealings

An 1859 drawing of Bent's Fort in Colorado. This fort was constructed by Bent in 1853 and replaced his older fort, which was in ruins.

between Plains Indians and white men. He also built a trading post, which was known as Bent's Fort.

Bent tried hard to encourage peace between the two sides. This was difficult, especially when the Cheyennes started attacking white settlements. In 1864 the governor of Colorado threatened to kill all American Indians found out on the Plains. Bent sent messages to the Cheyennes to come back to the safety of the reservation.

Bent was unable to stop the massacre at Sand Creek. But his three sons took part in the action—on different sides. Charles and George were living with their mother's people at the camp. Robert was a rancher, but he was forced to act as a guide for Chivington's troops.

Robert Bent later described some of the horrors of the massacre: "There were some thirty or forty squaws [American Indian women] collected in a hole for protection; they sent out a little girl about six years old with a white flag on a stick [a sign of surrender]; she had not proceeded a few steps before she was shot and killed. All the squaws in that hole were afterwards killed."[6]

WHAT HAPPENED AFTER SAND CREEK?

The massacre at Sand Creek shocked not only the Cheyennes, but also other Plains Indians as well. The survivors were joined by thousands of warriors from other American Indian groups. Among them were Sioux, Pawnee, Comanche, and Kiowa. This was the first time that Plains Indians had worked together to attack the whites. Soon, large bands were destroying settler and government property all over the Great Plains. Chivington's action had sparked all-out war.

Many whites, especially in the more liberal and "**civilized**" East, were also horrified by the Sand Creek savagery. Even Ulysses S. Grant, who was then a commander of the U.S. Army, called it "murder."[7]

There were two official investigations. One was made by the U.S. Congress, in response to criticism of the massacre across the nation. Several witnesses, including Robert Bent, presented Chivington in a negative light. Kit Carson, a famous trapper and guide, said the troops were "cowards and dogs."[8]

WAR ON THE PLAINS

The U.S. government offered to pay money to the survivors of the massacre. Chivington resigned from the Army. But these actions did not stop the fighting. On the central Plains, bands of Cheyennes, Sioux, and Arapahos continued raiding ranches and wagon trains. The town of Julesburg, in present-day Colorado, was burned down twice.[9]

The violence spread further north. In July 1865, a Plains Indian band attacked a military post at North Platte, in present-day Wyoming. They killed many men, including a wagonload of soldiers. Groups of U.S. soldiers set out to find the Sioux and Cheyenne war parties, but they were too late. The band of men had already left the area and gone north, into more remote country.

A NEW TREATY

By the fall of 1865, everyone had grown tired of the fighting. In October, the Bureau of Indian Affairs called a meeting with leaders from the Cheyennes and Arapahos to work out a new treaty. It took place near Wichita, Kansas. Black Kettle and other chiefs came, as well as trusted white men such as William Bent and Kit Carson.

The Civil War

Between 1861 and 1865, the United States was split by a bloody **civil war**. On one side was the Confederacy, made up of 11 southern states that wanted to keep the right to have slaves. On the other was the Union, consisting of the other states, most of which had banned slavery. The war ended in victory for the Union. The conflict had a big effect on the Plains Indian Wars, because many U.S. soldiers were taken away from the Plains, where they had been fighting Plains Indians, to fight instead in the war raging in the East.

War on two fronts

In the early 1860s, the United States was involved in two conflicts—the Civil War and the Plains Indians Wars. How did they compare in scale?

	Civil War	Plains Indian Wars
Combatants	Union: 2,100,000 Confederate: 900,000	U.S. Army: 30,000 Plains Indians (including older people, women, and children): 100,000
Deaths due to fighting	620,000	5,300
Bloodiest battle	Shiloh (1862): 23,700 dead	Little Bighorn (1876): 400

Sources: Clayton K. S. Chun, *The US Army in the Plains Indian Wars 1865-1891* (London: Osprey 2004), 34 Robert H. Lowie Indians of the Plains, 10 http://www.legendsofamerica.com/ah-civilwarfacts.html

The government agents said that the Cheyennes had to move again to a new reservation south of the Arkansas River, which they would have to share with another tribe, the Kiowas. "It will be a very hard thing to leave the country God gave us," said Chief Little Raven.[10] But the Cheyennes and Arapahos had little choice. They had lost many men, and they were exhausted by the fighting. So they agreed to the treaty, giving up all rights to their territory in Colorado.

RED CLOUD'S WAR

Peace could not last long, though, because the problems were still the same. Some white people now wanted to settle on the Plains, but most wanted to travel across them on their way to western destinations. Huge numbers of these people were headed for the gold fields in the hills of present-day Montana.

THE BOZEMAN TRAIL

To reach Montana, **prospectors** made a new road, which branched off northwest from the Oregon Trail. A miner named John Bozeman had created it in 1862, so it was called the Bozeman Trail.[1] Within a few years, thousands of prospectors were making the journey along it.

Unfortunately, the trail cut through some of the most important hunting grounds in the northern Plains. It crossed the Powder River, in present-day Montana and Wyoming, where the Lakota branch of the Sioux people lived and hunted buffalo. At first, the Sioux warned whites not to enter their territory. When this failed, they began attacking wagon trains.

FAILURE AT FORT LARAMIE

The white travelers demanded protection from the Sioux. So in 1866, the U.S. government decided to make the Bozeman Trail an official road. It would be guarded by regular troops, who would be stationed in a series of forts along the way. But first the Lakota had to be persuaded to stay peaceful.

Bureau agents invited Sioux leaders to Fort Laramie to discuss a new treaty. But the Sioux quickly realized that soldiers were already on their way to take over the trail. Most of the Sioux walked out of the talks. Chief Red Cloud (see box) said angrily: "Great Father [the U.S. president] sends us presents and wants new road. But White Chief goes with soldiers to steal road before Indian says yes or no."[2]

BUILDING THE FORTS

That year, the U.S. Army built three forts along the Bozeman Trail. The first of them was Fort Reno, in present-day Wyoming. This was a five-day ride (about 80 miles, or 128 kilometers) from the Platte River, the point where it branched from the Oregon Trail. Beyond these were Fort Phil Kearny, in present-day Wyoming, and Fort C. F. Smith, in present-day Montana. The men had to work quickly to make sure the buildings were ready before the harsh winter weather arrived.

This was a hard and dangerous life. For a start, there was the constant threat of raids by the Sioux. They stole horses, food, and equipment, they raided wagons, and they killed several men. The soldiers also had to make sure they had a good supply of food and water for the long cold months, as well as firewood and hay for the animals.

BIOGRAPHY

Red Cloud 1822–1909

BORN: Near the Platte River, in present-day Nebraska

ROLE: Lakota Sioux leader

Red Cloud's mother was from the Oglala branch of the Lakota tribe. As a young man, Red Cloud was a famous warrior in battles with neighboring Indians. In 1866 he led the fight against the U.S. Army's attempt to take control of the Powder River Country, near the Bozeman Trail (see pages 24 and 25). In 1868 the whites abandoned their forts there, and Red Cloud became the only American Indian to defeat the United States in war (see pages 28 and 29). Although he continued to argue for the rights of his people to their territories, he remained at peace with the whites for the rest of his long life.[3]

LIFE AT FORT PHIL KEARNY

Fort Phil Kearny was the biggest of the three forts. The soldiers were living in the wilderness, a long way from other white settlements. The fort had several buildings, including sleeping quarters, workshops, a hospital, and even a bandstand. These were surrounded by a **stockade** of wooden stakes sharpened at the top.[4]

Life was even more difficult for wives and children, who often joined soldiers at the forts. They rarely went outside the stockade, as Plains Indian attacks might come at any time. One officer's wife described the danger:

More than once the Sioux crawled up to the stockade covered with wolf skins and imitating the wolf cry, and on one occasion actually shot a sentry [guard] with an arrow that noiselessly pierced his heart.[5]

THE FETTERMAN MASSACRE

By December 1866, the three forts were complete. Meanwhile, a huge number of Sioux were gathering in the north. Bands from many different Sioux peoples had come to support Red Cloud and his Oglalas, as well as groups of Cheyennes and Arapahos. Soon their camps contained at least 4,000 warriors.

At Fort Phil Kearny there were fewer than 700 U.S. soldiers and male **civilians**. U.S. Army leaders realized the Sioux gathering was near, but they did not know how big it was. They also knew that the Plains Indians rarely had the patience to mount a long attack. On his side, Red Cloud accepted the fact that he could not capture the fort by force. So he decided to trick the white men out into the open and to attack them there.[6]

On December 21, a few Sioux warriors approached the fort, yelling and waving blankets. A force of about 80 soldiers left the fort to pursue them. The troops were led by William Fetterman, who had boasted that he could easily destroy the Sioux camp. As the Sioux ran away, Fetterman galloped after them.

The soldiers raced over a hilltop and straight into the Sioux trap. From all sides, hundreds of warriors came out of hiding and charged at them. The soldiers were outnumbered, and in a few minutes every one of them had been killed. It was the worst defeat the U.S. Army had yet suffered during its wars with the American Indians.

An 1877 print of the December 21, 1866 Fetterman Massacre at Fort Kearny.

BIOGRAPHY

William Tecumseh Sherman 1820–1891

BORN: Lancaster, Ohio

ROLE: Civil War hero and U.S. Army commander

William Tecumseh Sherman was one of the most successful Union generals during the Civil War. He was famous for his ruthless destruction of enemy cities and farmland. When the war ended, Sherman was appointed military commander for the land west of the Mississippi, which included the Great Plains.

Sherman continued with his brutal methods. Like many white leaders of the time, he believed the best way to make a lasting settlement alongside American Indians was to destroy them. After the Fetterman Massacre of 1866, Sherman wrote to President Ulysses S. Grant: "We must act with vindictive [vengeful] earnestness against the Sioux, even to their extermination—men, women and children."[7] But he later became less harsh in his dealings, and he was respected by many tribes for his good advice. The Plains Indians called Sherman "Great Warrior," because of his deeds in the Civil War.

THE WAGON BOX FIGHT

One of the strangest battles of the Plains Indian Wars took place in the summer of 1867. About 1,000 Sioux attacked 32 men from Fort Phil Kearny. Somehow, the U.S. soldiers held them off and lost only three men. How did they do it?

THE SETTING

About 6 miles (10 kilometers) from Fort Phil Kearny was a logging camp in the woods. Here men cut pine trees, which were hauled back to the fort to build walls and fences. Next to the camp was an oval corral made of 14 wagon boxes (the main bodies of wagons) pushed together. This barrier was made stronger in some places by logs. Mules and other animals were shut in the corral at night.[8]

THE TWO SIDES AND THE WEAPONS

The two sides of the battle were as follows:

- *Plains Indians*: The Oglala Sioux were probably led by Red Cloud. The exact number is unknown, but there were between 700 and 1,500.
- *Whites*: There were 32 men, made up of 2 officers, 24 troopers, and 6 civilians. The leader was Captain James W. Powell.[9]

The Sioux were armed mainly with bows and arrows, as well as knives and war clubs. It is possible that a few had rifles stolen from soldiers they had killed.

The soldiers had a surprise weapon—a new type of rifle. Before this time, the U.S. Army had used muzzle-loading guns. These were slow to reload, because the fresh cartridge had to be pushed down the muzzle (the end of the barrel) with a rod. Powell's men had brand-new breech-loading rifles. These could be reloaded quickly. The old cartridge was ejected, and a fresh one was pushed into the breech (above the trigger).[10]

THE FIGHT

When the Sioux attacked, the soldiers ran to the corral. They lay down with their rifles ready. Some fired through holes bored in the wagon boxes, while others fired through the gaps between the boxes. They had plenty of ammunition. They had piled up ox yokes, sacks of food, and salt barrels for extra protection.

The Sioux believed the whites were using muzzle-loaders. Once fired, they would take a while to reload. So the Sioux charged the corral on horseback, thinking they were safe from bullets after the first shot. But the new rifles kept up an almost continuous attack. Many Sioux were wounded or killed.

Confused, the Sioux retreated. They charged again on foot, and many almost reached the wagon boxes. But once again the deadly rifle fire forced them back. At last a rescue party of troops arrived from the fort, with a big howitzer (field gun). The Sioux retreated, this time for good.

About 60 of the Sioux were killed in the battle, while the U.S. Army lost only three.[11] But it was not a victory or a defeat for either side. This did not stop some whites from treating it as a triumph, especially after the horror of the Fetterman Massacre.

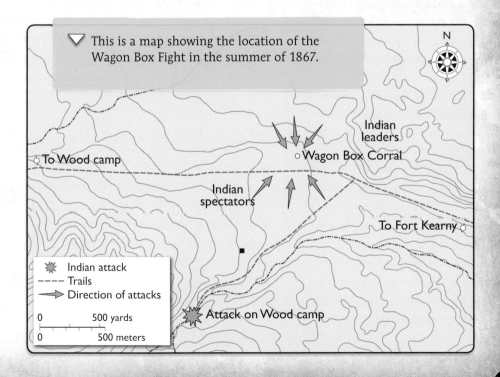

▽ This is a map showing the location of the Wagon Box Fight in the summer of 1867.

THE HIGH COST OF WAR

Conditions on the Bozeman Trail forts grew worse. In winter, supplies of food and firewood ran low. Horses, cattle, and other domestic animals starved, and men got sick because of the poor diet. In spring, the Sioux returned from their winter home to the south, and they began raiding again. Few whites dared to travel along the trail.

The U.S. government was anxious to find a way to settle the problem. It was clear that the Plains Indian Wars were very expensive. The Bureau of Indian Affairs calculated that the fighting since 1864 had cost the government $30 million (at least $3 billion in today's money).[12] And in spite of all this spending, the Army was unable to defeat or control Red Cloud and his forces.

The Medicine Lodge Treaty

While Red Cloud's war was still raging, other groups of American Indians further south had made a separate treaty with the whites. Leaders of the Comanches, Southern Cheyennes, Arapahos, and Kiowas assembled at Medicine Lodge, Kansas, in October 1867. They agreed to give up their tribal lands and move to smaller reservations in Oklahoma. In return, the government promised schools, houses, food, and training in farmwork. The Indians really wanted none of these things. They had given up farming long ago and become nomadic hunters. But the government was determined to make them live like white people.

In September 1867, General Sherman tried once more to make peace. He called a meeting at Platte City, Nebraska. Red Cloud refused to come, but other Sioux leaders were there. To their horror, Sherman warned that they would have to leave the Powder River and go to a new reservation near the Missouri River.

Sherman moved on to Fort Laramie, where he hoped the Sioux would agree to a treaty. This time, no Sioux came at all. But Red Cloud sent a message saying that he would talk peace when the soldiers left the forts. He added: "What I have said, I mean. I mean to keep this land."[13]

In April 1868, Sherman came back to Fort Laramie for yet more talks. A Bureau of Indian Affairs agent rode out to invite Red Cloud in person. The Sioux chief sent back this message: "We are on the mountain looking down on the soldiers and the forts. When we see the soldiers moving away and the forts abandoned, then I will come down and talk."[14]

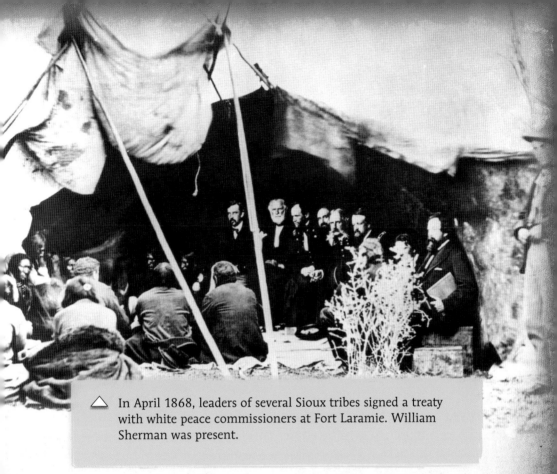

In April 1868, leaders of several Sioux tribes signed a treaty with white peace commissioners at Fort Laramie. William Sherman was present.

RED CLOUD MAKES PEACE

A month later, the U.S. government gave in. The soldiers marched out of Fort C. F. Smith. Red Cloud and his warriors immediately burned it down. The other two forts were also abandoned and destroyed. The Bozeman Trail itself was closed down for good.

At last, Red Cloud came down from the hills to sign the treaty at Fort Laramie. The government agreed that the Powder River Country belonged to the Sioux and their **allies**, and that whites were banned from going there without permission. Red Cloud promised to stop the war.

But as with most treaties made with the Plains Indians, most of the U.S. government's promises would be broken over the next 20 years. White miners and settlers would flood into the Powder River Country and beyond, and the government would not be able—or willing—to stop them. The Sioux would lose their hunting grounds and be confined to reservations elsewhere.

RED CLOUD IN WASHINGTON

In the spring of 1870, the great Sioux leader Red Cloud received a surprising invitation from the president, Ulysses S. Grant. Would he like to visit the "Great Father" (the American Indian name for the U.S. president) in his house in Washington, D.C.? Red Cloud was shocked at first. He had spent all his life on the wide-open spaces of the Plains, and he did not wish to make the long and tiring journey to a big city. But in the end he decided to go.

At this time, most Sioux were at peace with the whites. But violent actions by the U.S. Army had begun to change this. Many Plains Indians were growing rebellious. The government knew that Red Cloud was the most highly respected of the Sioux chiefs. They believed a trip to Washington would impress him with the power and achievements of the white people. They hoped he would go home and tell other chiefs that further violence would be useless.

Red Cloud himself was anxious to speak with President Grant. Sherman had said that the U.S. government wanted the Sioux to move to a new reservation on the Missouri River. Red Cloud wanted to explain that they did not want to leave the Powder River Country. It had been promised to them in the treaty.

GOING TO WASHINGTON

On May 26, Red Cloud and 15 other Oglala Sioux got into a special railroad car at Omaha Station, in Nebraska. They were amazed by the crowds of white people in Omaha, and by the noise and giant buildings in Chicago. The journey to Washington took five days—at a much faster speed than the men had ever traveled before.

The day after they arrived in Washington, the Sioux were given a tour of the city. They visited the Arsenal, where the U.S. Army manufactured and stored its weapons. Here they were shown a huge new cannon, which could fire a shell 4 miles (7 kilometers). Then they watched speakers in the Senate, which they found very dull, compared with their own debates back home.[15]

Red Cloud and his companions went to a grand party given by President Grant at the White House. They were not impressed by the important white guests, but they enjoyed the huge candle-lit chandeliers and the lavish food. Spotted Tail, another chief, pointed out: "Surely the white men have many more good things to eat than they send to the Indians."[16]

△ When the Sioux arrived in Washington, they were given "white men's clothes" to wear. But they disliked the tight-fitting coats and shoes. They were quickly given traditional American Indian clothing and moccasins, which they wore to the White House dinner.

But Red Cloud's main purpose in coming to Washington was to negotiate with the U.S. government. A few days later, he had a meeting with Grant. He told the president that his people did not want to move to the reservation near the Missouri River. In the end, the U.S. government gave in to his demands. The Sioux would be allowed to live on their old hunting grounds near Powder River. Red Cloud had won another victory.[17]

DEATH ON THE CENTRAL PLAINS

The great pioneer trails had brought huge disturbances to the Plains Indian way of life. But a new kind of transportation was going to make things much worse—the railroad.

In the early 1860s, the first rails were laid over the central Plains. One line, the Union Pacific, went west from Omaha, Nebraska. A second line, the Central Pacific, headed east from Sacramento, California. When they met, trains would be able to cross the continent.

WHAT CHANGES DID THE RAILROAD BRING?

Trains made the U.S. Army's work easier. They could carry troops, supplies, and equipment swiftly over long distances. This meant that many lonely forts near the railroad could be shut down, saving money and lives. The trains also brought huge numbers of settlers and traders to remote areas.

▽ The building of the railroad brought armies of laborers to the Great Plains, followed by buffalo hunters and settlers.

But for the American Indians who lived in the middle part of the Plains, the coming of the railroad was a disaster. The gangs of builders destroyed large areas of grassland. Hunters shot huge numbers of buffalo for food. The noise and smoke of the trains scared away other game animals.

Many Plains Indians still lived outside their reservations, where buffalo and game were easier to find. They preferred the free life of the wide-open spaces. Fearful of how the railroads were affecting their lifestyle, they began attacking railroad crews and trains themselves. They cut **telegraph** wires and killed **surveyors**. They put logs on the line or ripped up the rails, so the trains—or "iron horses," as they were called—crashed. Then they looted the wagons and boxcars.[2]

Rails across North America

In 1869 the Union Pacific and Central Pacific lines finally met. The site was Promontory Summit, in present-day Utah. On May 10 the joining ceremony took place. Locomotives from each company were drawn up facing each other. Then the final spikes were hammered in to fix the final rail ties. Two spikes were of gold, one was silver, and the hammer itself had a silver head. For the first time, a railroad linked the West Coast and the East Coast of the United States.[1]

But the track-laying gangs were enormous. As they moved across the land, they were followed by huge camps with saloons, stores, and gambling dens. And they were well protected. At least 5,000 soldiers guarded the line, as well as bands of American Indians who had agreed to work for the whites.[3]

WINTER KILLINGS

General Sherman was determined to sweep the remaining American Indians off the central Plains. "We have provided reservations for all," he said. "All who cling to their old hunting grounds are hostile and remain so till killed off." He ordered a ruthless campaign against Indian villages outside reservations in the winter of 1868.

On November 27, 1868, **cavalry** troops led by General George Armstrong Custer found a Cheyenne village by the Washita River, in present-day Oklahoma. These Indians, led by Black Kettle, were peaceful—but off their reservation. Custer's men charged, destroying the village and killing over 100 Cheyennes. Many of these people were survivors from the Sand Creek Massacre (see page 17).[4]

LIFE IN A FRONTIER TOWN

As more pioneers arrived, settlements grew up on the empty Plains. They often started as simple trading posts. Trappers brought in furs, meat, and buffalo skins, farmers brought in grain and other produce, and miners brought in gold dust. They traded these for the goods they needed, such as food, ammunition, and clothes.

LAW AND ORDER

Frontier towns could be wild and violent places. Cow herders and miners worked very hard for long hours and often in uncomfortable conditions. They liked to enjoy themselves on their days off, especially if they had just been paid. They drank a lot of cheap whisky, danced, gambled, and visited **brothels**.

Not surprisingly, fights were common. As many cowboys carried weapons, these might turn into gunfights. Most big towns were also centers of crime. Thieves were attracted by the gold and silver from mines, or by the cattle.

Frontier towns like this in Tomapah, Nevada, grew up fast and attracted settlers to the West.

Women in the West

Men who made long journeys and settled in the West had to be tough. Women often had to be even tougher. In addition to usual household chores, they had to chop wood, handle horses, and carry water. And, of course, they gave birth to and raised children. Living on isolated farms, they could be alone all day. In some areas, there was the threat of attacks by Plains Indians or thieves.

Many girls moved to the nearest town as soon as they could. Here they might find work or a husband more easily. Many women also founded schools and churches and campaigned against drunkenness and the mistreatment of American Indians.[5]

A town's chief law officer was the federal marshal. Many successful marshals became legendary figures of the West, such as Wild Bill Hickok (in Abilene, Kansas) and Wyatt Earp (in Dodge City, Kansas). But many settlements had no law officers. If there was no marshal, some townspeople formed their own groups to punish criminals.

WHAT WAS IN TOWNS?

Frontier towns varied greatly in size, from tiny outposts with only one store, to bigger settlements with 100 or more inhabitants and many facilities. The following features were found in most towns:

- *The store*: The store sold all the essentials for frontier living— anything from cloth and coffee to nails and rifle cartridges.
- *The express office*: The express office was the place to take or collect mail. Companies like Wells Fargo carried mail to remote camps and towns by pony or wagon.
- *The hotel*: The hotel was often the only place to stay in town and get a meal.
- *The saloon*: The saloon was where most drinking and gambling took place. Saloons were often bright and glittering places, and they attracted local men in search of excitement and glamour.
- *The bank*: The bank was mainly a secure room where people's cash and gold were stored more safely than they would be at home.
- *The forge*: The forge was often the only factory in town, where the blacksmith made simple iron tools, utensils, and horseshoes.
- *The butcher's shop*: The butcher's shop sold a lot of wild meat, such as bear, buffalo, antelope, and prairie chicken.[6]

"THE ONLY GOOD INDIAN IS A DEAD INDIAN"

By the fall of 1869, the U.S. Army had almost completed its mission to drive the American Indians off the central area of the Plains, between the Platte and Arkansas rivers. Most Indians had been forced to move back to their reservations. A few Cheyennes and Arapahos had fled further West, where there were fewer white settlers, and there was enough wilderness for them to hide.

The majority of the tribes knew they had no choice but to give in to the soldiers. They could not compete with the numbers and firepower of the enemy. One Comanche chief surrendered to General Philip Sheridan, saying he was a "good Indian." Sheridan replied: "The only good Indians I ever saw were dead."[7] This became a phrase used by whites all over the West.

BIOGRAPHY

Ulysses S. Grant

1822–1885

BORN: Point Pleasant, Ohio

ROLE: U.S. Army commander and 18th president of the United States

Ulysses S. Grant showed himself to be a brilliant soldier in the Civil War, and he became commander of the Union Army in 1864. He was elected president of the United States in 1868. Grant wanted to find a peaceful way to deal with American Indians. However, he found it hard to keep complete control of his forces on the Plains, when he was so far away in Washington, D.C. One of his first acts was to reform the Bureau of Indian Affairs. He encouraged religious organizations such as the Quakers to take over local agencies on the reservations. He was reelected president in 1872.[8]

THE MASSACRE GOES ON

Soon many Plains Indians had surrendered and were at peace. Those who stayed out of the reservations were assumed to be hostile, so they were treated with great savagery by U.S. troops. The winter killings continued. In January 1870, soldiers found a camp of Piegans (Blackfeet) in present-day Montana. The Blackfeet were friendly, but the troops still slaughtered them, killing over 170 people, most of them women and children.[9]

Some bands of Comanches and Kiowas continued fighting near the Texas border. In 1871 U.S. soldiers arrested their leaders, who were put on trial for murder and sentenced to be hanged. There were strong protests against this in the East, and the chiefs were released two years later.

Did you know?

For such a famous soldier, Grant had a bad start to his military career. In 1854 he was forced to resign from the U.S. Army because of his drunkenness.

NO MORE TREATIES

In 1871 the U.S. Congress passed a law that made a big change to the way the government treated American Indians. The Indian Appropriations Act ruled that the tribes or nations were no longer separate and self-governing groups. Instead, they were regarded as a single, independent nation.

In the previous 100 years, the government had made 371 treaties with different tribes. The new law meant this would not happen anymore. Instead of treaties, the government would make laws and orders that applied to all Indians equally.[10] This was deliberately intended to break up the tribal structure, by treating American Indians as individuals rather than members of a specific tribe or nations.

VANISHING HERDS

Hunting buffalo was central to the lives of most Plains Indians. They depended on these animals for food and many other materials. In the Medicine Lodge Treaty of 1867 (see page 29), they had been promised the right to hunt buffalo over a large area. In the early 1870s, there were still huge herds of buffalo on the Great Plains. But they were beginning to disappear—very quickly (see page 40).

WHO KILLED THE BUFFALO?

Who killed the buffalo? Several groups were responsible:

- *American Indians*: Plains tribes such as the Sioux killed many buffalo. But compared with white hunters, their total slaughter was small. More than 3 million buffalo were killed between 1872 and 1874. Indians killed only about 150,000 of them.[1]
- *Railroad builders*: Hunters shot buffalo to provide meat for the huge armies of laborers as they moved across the Plains.
- *Sportsmen*: Wealthy hunters came from the East and even from abroad for the excitement of shooting these large animals.
- *Railroad passengers*: Enormous herds of buffalo would sometimes block the way of trains. Passengers fired wildly into the buffalo, in an attempt to clear them away. In one instance, near Dodge City, Kansas, passengers killed more than 500.[2]
- *Hide hunters*: By 1872 buffalo hide had become valuable, as it was used for making shoes, belts, and other expensive goods. Hundreds of professional hunters came to the Plains. Buffalo were easy to shoot, and many hunters killed more than 100 a day.[3]

MORE BROKEN PROMISES

The destruction of the buffalo herds was a bitter blow for the Plains Indians. Many went hungry because there were suddenly not enough animals to provide meat. Worse still, if they could not find buffalo, there was no reason for them to stay in their tribal hunting grounds. The buffalo was an essential part of the Plains Indian way of life, and of the land on which these peoples lived. The promise of the Medicine Lodge Treaty now seemed worthless.

At the same time, the flow of white settlers on the Plains had become a flood.

Under the Homestead Act of 1862, anyone who laid claim to 160 acres (65 hectares) of land could file a patent after five years.[4] Throughout the early 1870s, thousands of pioneers became **homesteaders** west of the Mississippi River—often on territory promised to Indians.

Cattle drives

In the 1860s, a new kind of animal herd appeared on the grasslands. This was the longhorn cow. Cattle had been driven across parts of the Plains before, but now huge herds appeared. Gangs of riders, called cowboys, drove as many as 4,000 cattle north from Mexico and Texas. The slow journeys could take nearly four months. The cattle plodded as far north as Montana, or to Kansas, where they were loaded into railroad trucks. They were taken to the cities of the East, where there was a huge demand for fresh meat to feed the quickly growing population.

By the mid-1870s, large herds of buffalo had all but disappeared from the Great Plains.

THE BUFFALO

For Plains Indians, the most important animal on the Great Plains was the buffalo. It gave them food, shelter, clothing, and was an important part in their religious beliefs. Their summers were spent following and hunting the buffalo herds.

HOW MANY BUFFALO WERE THERE?

Long ago, the buffalo roamed across much of North America. By the time the Plains Indian Wars began, the herds were mostly confined to the Plains region. There were probably more than 60 million of them. Then the European hunters arrived. By the time the wars ended in 1890, there were hardly any buffalo left.

It was easy for a hunter armed with a rifle to kill a buffalo. A bull buffalo stood over 6 feet (2 meters) high and weighed about 2,000 pounds (900 kilograms). It was shortsighted, but it had strong senses of smell and hearing.[5]

WHAT WAS THE BUFFALO USED FOR?

How did Plains Indians use the buffalo?

- *Food*: Buffalo meat was a major part of the Plains Indians' diet. They cooked and ate some fresh meat, and they preserved the rest by drying. They sliced the meat, dried it in the sun, and then pounded and mixed it with fat and crushed wild cherries. This was called pemmican.[6]
- *Clothing*: Plains Indians hung the hide out to dry in the sun, scraping off the hair and the fat. They used the hide to make moccasins, robes, and leggings.
- *Shelter*: Plains Indians used whole hides as the coverings for tipis. They also made hides into buckets, cradles, and many other household items.
- *Weapons*: Plains Indians also made buffalo hide into shields and sheaths for knives. The strings of bows were usually the **sinews** from the hind legs. Sinews were also used to strengthen the bow handles and give them more spring.[7]
- *Other uses*: Plains Indians twisted buffalo hair into rope or used it to create fringe on headdresses. They boiled hooves to make glue. They also carved horns into spoons, cups, and toys.

THE BUFFALO AND RELIGION

The Sioux believed that the gods had given them the buffalo as a means of staying alive. The return of the buffalo herds in spring was seen as part of the unchanging cycle of life on Earth. They even believed that buffalo were born out of the soil itself—a symbol of the link between the animals and the Plains. If the buffalo disappeared, the land had no value for the Plains Indians.[8]

Did you know?

Before the Plains Indians had horses and guns, hunting buffalo was not as easy or quick. One way to kill them was to drive the herd into a narrow valley leading to a cliff. The buffaloes fell off the edge and died. Another method was to trap them in an enclosed space, and then spear or shoot them.

▽ The Plains Indians cut up buffalo meat, then spread it on racks to dry out in the sun. This prevented the meat from going bad.

ATTACKING THE HIDE HUNTERS

The Plains Indians on the southern Plains hated the buffalo hunters. These hunters were destroying the **sacred** herds and making food scarce for the native peoples. On top of this, once they had removed the hides, white hunters left the **carcasses** to rot. Large areas of the Plains were covered with the stinking remains.

Comanche and Kiowa warriors made frequent attacks on the camps of the hunters. But they soon realized that the white men were moving further south. There were simply too few buffalo left in Kansas and Colorado. So the hunters were heading for Texas.

THE TEXAS PANHANDLE

Buffalo were still plentiful in the Texas Panhandle. This is a square region in the northern corner of the state of Texas. The first hide hunters arrived there in 1874 and began shooting. A trading post was built near the Red River. It became known as Adobe Walls.

However, according to the Medicine Lodge Treaty, this was Indian Country—the hunting grounds of several tribes. White men were forbidden from hunting there. Several Kiowas and Comanches decided they must fight for their land, or lose it altogether. In June 1874 they attacked Adobe Walls, only to be beaten back by the power of the hide hunters' rifles.

BIOGRAPHY

Satanta, or White Bear 1820–1878

ROLE: Kiowa chief

Satanta grew up to be an exceptionally strong man, and he was famous as a warrior among the Kiowa. He became a chief in 1866. After the failure of the Medicine Lodge Treaty, he and his people went to live on a reservation. But soon the Kiowa grew tired of living on government handouts, and so they moved back to the Plains.

In 1871 Satanta led attacks on wagon trains, and he was soon arrested by soldiers and imprisoned. After being released two years later, he continued to lead attacks on settlements. He was jailed again, and in 1878 he killed himself by jumping through an upstairs prison window.[9]

THE RED RIVER WAR

After the failure of this raid, many southern Plains Indians decided to surrender and go back to the reservations. But others continued hunting, angry that the promise of the treaty had been broken yet again. That fall a large band of Comanches, Kiowas, and Cheyennes was camped in a hidden canyon in the middle of the panhandle.

General Sherman saw this as the ideal chance to clear all Indians off the southern Plains. He sent five **columns** of troops into the panhandle. One of these attacked the camps in September 1874. The Indians fled, leaving all their possessions. The U.S. Army then destroyed everything in the camp, including 1,400 horses.[10]

▽ General Sherman proved himself to be a ruthless fighter during the Civil War, when he destroyed the enemy's food stores and infrastructure.

The Indians had nowhere to run. They were cold, starving, and surrounded by soldiers. Over the next few months, the troops hunted them down, forcing the bands to surrender. At last, in June 1875, the final party of Comanches laid down its weapons. These people's days of freedom on the southern Plains were over for good, and they returned to their reservation.[11]

THE BLACK HILLS

Meanwhile, another war between U.S. forces and American Indians was boiling up further north. After the Fort Laramie Treaty of 1868 (see page 29), many Sioux stayed in the Powder River region, in present-day Montana and Wyoming, where they could live in the traditional way. Red Cloud and his people went to live on the Sioux reservation in present-day South Dakota. This included an area of small mountains called the Black Hills.

PAHA SAPA

The Black Hills ("Paha Sapa" in the Sioux language) were a sacred place for the Lakota Sioux and other tribes. They believed that gods and other spirits lived there. American Indians went there to speak with the spirits and receive **visions**.[1]

But the Black Hills were important for another reason. More rain fell there, so grass and other plants grew quickly. Trees were plentiful, and they could be used for firewood or making tipis. There was a good supply of small game animals and birds in the small valleys. The Sioux leader Sitting Bull called the Hills a "food pack."[2]

△ George Custer led the first white expedition into the Black Hills to look for gold. One of Custer's camps is shown here.

GOLD!

In July 1874, a white **expedition** made its way into the Black Hills. General Custer led the column of troops, wagons, and scouts. This mission had two aims: to look for a site for a new army fort, and to find gold. Many people believed the Hills were rich in gold deposits.

Very soon the soldiers found gold. When the news came out, prospectors raced to find their fortunes in present-day North Dakota and South Dakota. Sherman ordered troops to stop this new gold rush, but it was too late. By the end of 1875, there were over 15,000 miners in the Black Hills.[3]

The Sioux were outraged at this illegal invasion of their land. One of their leaders, Sitting Bull (see box), said: "Only seven years ago we made a treaty by which we were assured that the buffalo country should be left to us forever. Now they threaten to take that away from us."[4]

Red Cloud complained to the Bureau of Indian Affairs. In reply, the government sent a commission to persuade the Indians to sell the Black Hills. The Sioux, led by Sitting Bull, angrily refused. A young chief named Crazy Horse (see pages 46 and 47) said: "One does not sell the earth upon which the people walk."[5] Warriors began chanting a new song: "The Black Hills is my home and I love it, and whoever interferes will hear this gun."[6]

BIOGRAPHY

Sitting Bull 1831–1890

BORN: Grand River, in present-day South Dakota

ROLE: Lakota holy man and chief

Sitting Bull's name in Sioux was Tatanka-Iyotanka, which means "a bull sitting defiantly on its haunches." He fought in his first battle at the age of 14. By the early 1870s, he was one of the main chiefs of the Sioux.

Sitting Bull led the resistance to the sale of the Black Hills, and he played a major part in the victory at the Little Bighorn (see page 49). After this, he led his people to Canada to escape from U.S. troops. He returned in 1881 and took part in Buffalo Bill Cody's "Wild West Show" (see pages 54 and 55). Sitting Bull was killed in 1890, during a fight with police who had come to arrest him.[7]

CRAZY HORSE

Crazy Horse had a short life. He died in his mid-thirties. Yet today he is still seen as the greatest of all the Sioux war heroes. He was not only a fierce and fearless warrior, but also a brilliant leader of men in battle. His skill and ferocity helped to inspire the most famous American Indian victory during the Plains Wars, at the Battle of the Little Bighorn in 1876 (see page 49).

EARLY LIFE

Crazy Horse was born about 1840 at Bear Butte, in present-day South Dakota. He was one of the group of Sioux called the Oglalas. His father was a healer and holy man who explained people's dreams.[8]

Crazy Horse inherited some of his father's gifts, though he proved himself to be a man of action. He quickly learned to ride and went with his father on buffalo hunts. At the age of only 13, he took part in a horse-stealing raid on some neighboring Indians.[9]

CRAZY HORSE'S DREAM

At this time, the Sioux seldom saw white people. But soon Crazy Horse had his first experience of white violence. In 1854 he was present when U.S. soldiers attacked a Sioux camp, killing one of the chiefs. The Indians fought back and massacred the troops.

The incident affected Crazy Horse deeply. He started having visions. One day he rode out of camp alone on a "vision quest" (a search for a mystical turning point in an American Indian child's life). For three days he sat on a hilltop without food or water. In a dream he saw a warrior on horseback, who told him how to decorate his body with war paint in a special way. He warned him not to take scalps. In this way, he would not be harmed by bullets or arrows.[11]

Did you know?

There are no photographs of Crazy Horse. He always refused to pose for a camera. The only picture of him that exists is a sketch made long after his death. The artist got the details from Crazy Horse's sister in 1934.[10]

SURRENDER AND DEATH

When U.S. troops, under General George Crook, invaded the Black Hills in 1876, Crazy Horse led the Indian resistance. He drove back the soldiers at Rosebud Creek, in present-day Montana. Eight days later, his warriors made a charge, surrounding and destroying a column of the 7th Cavalry led by General George Custer, at the Little Bighorn.

Crazy Horse was arrested in September 1877. At first, he was calm. But when he knew he was going to prison, he struggled to escape. A trooper stabbed him with a bayonet (a kind of blade attached to a rifle). Crazy Horse died that night.

THE CRAZY HORSE MEMORIAL

Crazy Horse has become a legend. In 1948 Polish-American sculptor Korczak Ziólkowski began carving a huge statue of the Oglala warrior, seated on a horse and pointing. The carving was in the solid rock of Thunderhead Mountain in the Black Hills. It is still unfinished today.

▽ Work on the enormous Crazy Horse memorial sculpture is still unfinished after more than 60 years.

THE WAR FOR THE BLACK HILLS

Since the Sioux refused to sell the Black Hills, the U.S. government decided to take the hills by force. In the late spring of 1876, three columns of soldiers set off from different bases. One, commanded by General Alfred Terry, included Custer's cavalry. The others were under General George Crook (see box) and Colonel John Gibbon. The aim was to meet in the Black Hills and drive the tribes out.

BIOGRAPHY

George Crook 1829–1890

BORN: Taylorsville, Ohio

ROLE: U.S. military commander in the Sioux Wars

General George Crook fought on the Union side in the Civil War. In 1866 he began his long career fighting against American Indians, serving in present-day Idaho and Arizona before being sent to command the U.S. Army on the central Plains in 1875. The Apaches and other American Indians called Crook "Chief Gray Wolf," because of his cunning. He led the disastrous expedition to the Black Hills, and he later supervised the moving of the Sioux onto reservations. But the Indians trusted him, because he treated them honestly and kept many of his promises. Red Cloud said, "He never lied to us. His words gave the people hope."[12] In 1886 Crook helped persuade the Apache leader Geronimo to make peace.

Crook was the first to meet the Plains Indians. A band of Lakotas and Cheyennes surprised his column near Rosebud Creek on June 17. Crazy Horse led the riders, shouting: "Come on, Dakotas [Sioux]! It's a good day to die!"[13] The soldiers were shocked by the violence of the charge, but they managed to fight off the attack.

Meanwhile, General Terry had reports that Sitting Bull's camp was near the Little Bighorn River. He sent Gibbon's column to the north. Custer, with his 600 cavalry, was ordered to find the camp and attack from the south. Terry hoped this would drive the Sioux up the valley, where they would run into Gibbon's column.

As Custer set off on June 22, Gibbon said, "Now Custer, don't be greedy, but wait for us." Custer just waved and rode away. He arrogantly believed the 7th Cavalry could defeat the Indians all on its own. He drove his men at top speed toward the Little Bighorn Valley.[14]

CUSTER'S LAST STAND

Sitting Bull's camp was much larger than Terry or Custer realized. It now stretched for 3 miles (4.8 kilometers) and contained more than 6,000 Plains Indians. In addition to the different Sioux peoples, there were Blackfoot and Cheyenne. At least 2,000 of these were warriors.[15]

On June 25, Custer saw the camp, but he was unable to see how big it was. He decided to attack at once, before Terry's force arrived and before Gibbon had reached his position further north. Custer was determined to win all the glory for himself. He divided his troops into three groups—one to the left and one in the middle, while Custer advanced to the right.

All three parties ran into huge numbers of warriors. Custer and his 225 troops, trapped on a ridge, were surrounded. The Indians killed every single man. The other two parties lost about 40 men before they were rescued by the arrival of General Terry. The Sioux had won their greatest victory. It was also their last.

▽ Custer (kneeling, left) during his last stand.

GEORGE ARMSTRONG CUSTER

General George Armstrong Custer is one of the best-known figures in U.S. history. He was a dashing cavalry officer who wore his own colorful uniform and had long, curly golden hair. He showed himself to be a brave and inspiring leader. But today he is famous for only one reason—his disastrous defeat and death at the Battle of the Little Bighorn in 1876 (see page 49).

THE DASHING CAVALRY OFFICER

Custer was born in New Rumley, Ohio, in 1839. He went to West Point military academy, where he was lazy and ended up at the bottom of his class. But during the Civil War he became a hero of the Union side. He was dynamic and willing to take risks. His greatest moment came in 1863 at Gettysburg, Pennsylvania, when he led a charge that broke a major Confederate attack.

In 1866 he was appointed lieutenant-colonel of the 7th Cavalry, and he led its campaign against the Cheyennes. His massacre of over 100 Cheyennes on the Washita River in 1868 (see page 33) won him more fame. He was promoted to the rank of general. But Custer's arrogant ways often got him into trouble with his superiors.

His behavior even enraged President Grant, who took away Custer's command in 1876.[16] This meant Custer would miss the planned military expedition to drive the Sioux from the Black Hills. Custer was deeply upset. He went to see General Terry. Falling to his knees, he begged him to help. In the end, the president changed his mind, and Custer joined the expedition.[18]

Did you know?

Custer loved military music. So he took a 16-man band with him on the 1876 Black Hills expedition. He would sometimes stop and make the musicians climb up a hill and play a tune. However, before they reached the Black Hills, General Terry ordered that the band should be left behind.[17]

WHY DID CUSTER DIE AT THE LITTLE BIGHORN?

Custer's cavalry was part of a force of nearly 2,000 soldiers. Sitting Bull and his camp had almost the same number of warriors. Yet Custer's unit was massacred—largely due to his mistakes:

- Custer and his 600 men were far ahead of the main part of the army. He attacked without waiting for the rest to get into position.
- His men were very tired, having ridden at full speed for five days. He did not allow them any rest.
- He did not bother to find out exactly how many Indian warriors there were. He thought there were only a few hundred in the camp.
- He split his force into three parts. Custer was left with only 225 men in his own unit. This made it easy for Sitting Bull and his camp to surround and overwhelm them.[19]

▽ In the early 1870s, Custer (pictured left) escorted the Russian Grand Duke Alexis Romanov on a buffalo hunting expedition in Nebraska.

LOST HOMELANDS

The news of Custer's defeat in the Black Hills took a while to reach the rest of the United States. Most people heard it in early July, when they were celebrating the Fourth of July. The disaster shocked the nation. This time there was no sympathy for the cause of the American Indians, as there had been after the Sand Creek Massacre. Now most white Americans wanted revenge.

CLEARING THE BLACK HILLS

The first step toward revenge was a new law. In August 1876, the U.S. government ordered the Plains Indians to give up all their claims to the Black Hills and the Powder River Country. This act once again broke the Fort Laramie Treaty of 1868. So there was a new treaty to replace it. Most of the chiefs signed it, including Red Cloud.[1]

The second step was military action. In November 1876, two big new expeditions set out to subdue the Sioux. One was commanded by Colonel Nelson Miles, the other by General Crook. They destroyed Indian villages and drove the survivors onto their reservations. By May, even Crazy Horse had surrendered. Four months later, he was dead.

Only one great Sioux leader escaped the revenge campaign—Sitting Bull. But he was no longer in the Black Hills. Tired of being chased by soldiers, he and his followers had gone north and crossed the border into Canada. This was British territory, where the Sioux could live outside the reach of the U.S. Army. There were fewer white settlers in large areas of western Canada, so there was room for the Sioux to live peacefully.

THE EPIC OF THE NEZ PERCÉ

Few bands of American Indians stayed free for long. One of these was the Nez Percé, who lived in the beautiful Wallowa Valley in Oregon. For years they had remained peaceful, even though white settlers poured into their lands. In 1877 the U.S. government ordered them to move to a reservation in present-day Idaho.

One of the Nez Percé leaders was Chief Joseph. He refused to be confined on a reservation. With about 250 men, women, and children, he set off eastward in June 1877 to escape the soldiers. Thus began an amazing journey. For over five months, the starving Nez Percés managed to fight off a force of over 5,000 troops. Chief Joseph finally surrendered in October, as winter approached. The Nez Percés moved to their new reservation with great sadness.[2]

Upon surrendering on October 5, 1877, Chief Joseph made the following speech:

I am tired of fighting. Our chiefs are killed.... It is cold and we have no blankets. The little children are freezing to death. My people, some of them have run away to the hills.... I want to have time to look for my children and see how many I can find. Maybe I shall find them among the dead. Hear me, my chiefs, I am tired. My heart is sick and sad. From where the sun now stands, I will fight no more forever.[3]

▷ Despite his heroic and gallant journey, Chief Joseph was never allowed to return to his beloved Wallowa Valley home.

53

BUFFALO BILL'S "WILD WEST SHOW"

Sitting Bull worked for Buffalo Bill's Wild West Show for a short time, but gave all his wages away to beggars.

William "Buffalo Bill" Cody (1846–1917) led a colorful life. He was a hunter, a scout, a fur trapper, a soldier, a gold miner, an actor, and a Pony Express rider. (The Pony Express was a mail delivery service that used mail carriers on horseback.)

But Cody became famous all over the United States and Europe for his "Wild West Show," which reenacted famous episodes from the exciting days of the old history of the West. The show was hugely popular, in part because many people knew little about these events. By the 1880s most of the frontier regions had been tamed and settled, and most American Indians had been placed into reservations, with no more war. The stories of bandits, warriors, massacres, and sharpshooters became part of legend—which the "Wild West Show" helped to create.

A WESTERN LEGEND

Cody got his nickname when he worked as a buffalo hunter. In the late 1860s, he shot buffalo to provide meat for the men building the railroad in Kansas. At the same time "Buffalo Bill" was a scout for the U.S. Army and took part in many battles against the Indians.

He liked to show off, wearing his golden hair long and wearing fine clothes. He also enjoyed acting. In 1873 he appeared in a play called *The Scouts of the Plains*—playing himself. Also in the cast was the lawman and gunfighter "Wild Bill" Hickok.[4]

WHAT WOULD YOU HAVE SEEN IN THE "WILD WEST SHOW"?

Buffalo Bill launched his spectacular show in 1883, calling it "America's National Entertainment."[5] Over the years he built up a cast of hundreds of men and women, as well as a huge variety of animals. They appeared in reimagined scenes from western history. Among these were a buffalo hunt, a train robbery, and "Indian" horse races. The climax was a re-creation of Custer's "last stand" at the Little Bighorn.

There were also displays of frontier skills such as shooting and lassoing. And, of course, there was horse riding. The riders included U.S. cavalrymen and American Indians, as well as horseback warriors from other cultures, including German soldiers, Mexican vaqueros, Russian Cossacks, Arabs, Cubans, and even Pacific Islanders.[6] Of course, Cody's picture of the Old West and its characters was not entirely accurate. He took many liberties with history in order to make his show more glamorous and sensational.

FAMOUS NAMES

The following are some of the stars who appeared in Buffalo Bill's "Wild West Show":
- *Annie Oakley*: Nicknamed "Little Sure Shot," Annie Oakley performed amazing feats with a rifle and pistol. She could hit a thrown playing card five times before it reached the floor, and she once knocked the ash off a cigarette held by the king of Germany.
- *Sitting Bull*: The Sioux leader Sitting Bull was a friend of Cody. He was employed in 1885 to ride round the ring once, and then sign autographs.
- *Short Bull*: A Lakota Sioux, Short Bull was an important figure in the spread of the Ghost Dance (see page 61). He joined the show in 1891 and even visited Europe with it.

THE END OF THE PLAINS INDIANS

The year 1877 saw the U.S. Army sweep almost all American Indians from the open Plains. The Sioux and other American Indians groups seemed to have lost their struggle to live and hunt freely. They now lived on reservations. The Sioux nation was confined inside present-day North Dakota and South Dakota. The Cheyennes, the Arapahos, and the Nez Percés were in present-day Oklahoma.

There was now peace over most of the region—for the first time since the early 1860s. White settlements grew rapidly. Roads, railroads, and cattle ranches began to cover the grasslands. But the Plains Indian Wars were not quite finished.

THE FLIGHT OF THE CHEYENNES

The Northern Cheyennes hated their new home. There were very few buffalo, and diseases such as **malaria** were widespread. They longed for their old land, in present-day Montana. In September 1878, about 300 of them left the reservation and set off northward.

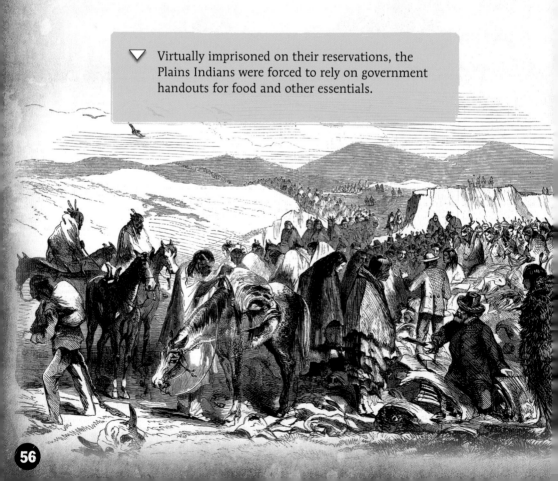

▽ Virtually imprisoned on their reservations, the Plains Indians were forced to rely on government handouts for food and other essentials.

Fencing the Great Plains

Ranchers needed fences to keep their livestock from roaming. But there was no timber for fencing on the Plains. Then, in the 1870s, an Illinois farmer invented a new kind of wire with barbs (sharp points) in it. By 1880 he had a factory that produced 600 miles (960 kilometers) of barbed wire a day. Soon, large parts of the Great Plains were fenced off with wire. This invention changed the face of the Old West.[7]

Soldiers came after these Cheyennes. The Cheyennes fought them off in a series of running battles, then split into two parties. One, led by Dull Knife, was captured, but it managed to fight its way free again. The chase went on through the bitter snow of the winter. When the Cheyennes finally surrendered, only 78 of them were still alive.[8]

THE RETURN OF SITTING BULL

Sitting Bull was now the only great Plains Indian leader who had not made peace. But he too was unhappy away from home. Canada was cold and unfriendly, and game was hard to find. At last, in July 1881, Sitting Bull and his followers moved back across the border into the United States and surrendered.

Sitting Bull was held as a prisoner of the U.S. Army for more than a year. In 1883 he was released and sent to the Standing Rock Indian Reservation, in present-day North Dakota and South Dakota. He was old and poor, and he remembered the past with sadness. "A warrior I have been," he said. "Now it is all over. A hard time I have."[9]

THE LAST BUFFALO HUNT

Soon after Sitting Bull arrived at Standing Rock, he led his warriors out to hunt buffalo. The huge herds of the southern Plains had been wiped out by white hunters, but a few were left in the northern Plains. Within a short time, the Sioux had killed most of these. The days of buffalo hunting were over. The Great Plains were given over to cattle and crop fields.[10]

LAND RUSH

Throughout the 1880s, the number of white settlers coming west grew enormously. Besides white Americans, there were thousands of pioneers pouring in from Great Britain and other parts of northern Europe. Many of these reached the Missouri River and the central and eastern parts of the Dakotas—the border of the Great Sioux Reservation and the remains of the old Indian Territory. American Indians would have to be moved yet again to make room.

TRIBAL BREAKDOWN

In 1887 the U.S. Congress passed a new law called the Dawes Act. This split up the reservations. The American Indians' land went from being large areas of land held by groups to small units owned by individual people.[1] The law was aimed at breaking up the communal life of the Indians and encouraging them to mix into white society.

But the Dawes Act had another effect. After dividing the reservations, government agents could set aside areas of land for settlers. In this way, Indian land was gradually eaten away. American Indians were crowded into smaller spaces. Another treaty promise was broken.

The Indians themselves were unhappy with this forced breakup of their old ways. But white settlers were glad to have more land, and white politicians saw the Dawes Act as a fresh start. One said: "The Indian may now become a free man; free from the thralldom [bondage] of the tribe; freed from the domination of the reservation system; free to enter into the body of our citizens."[2]

The Indian Territory had been promised permanently to American Indians back in 1830. Now most of it was about to disappear. In 1887 the U.S. Congress voted to allow settlers to move into large parts of the territory, in present-day Oklahoma.

On April 22, 1889, at least 50,000 pioneers lined up for the first great "land rush." Pistol shots signaled the start, and they rushed forward on carts, horseback, bicycles, and foot to claim their piece of land. By nightfall, nearly 2 million acres (809,000 hectares) of Indian Territory had been grabbed.[3] More land rushes were to follow.

SPLITTING THE SIOUX

In 1887 Buffalo Bill Cody had asked Sitting Bull to appear in his "Wild West Show" again. Sitting Bull refused, saying, "I am needed here. There is more talk of grabbing our lands."[4] He knew the government was planning to take away part of the Sioux reservation and open it to white settlers.

In 1889 General Crook came to the reservation. He offered the Sioux leaders $1.50 per acre for their land. This was probably less than the real value, but better than the 50 cents per acre the U.S. government had offered a year before. He told them that the white people "come west. And they are still coming, and will come until they overrun all of this country. And you can't prevent it."[6] Most of the chiefs signed the treaty agreeing to split their land. Sitting Bull was one of the few who refused.

▽ The last great land rush took place in 1893. In one day, over 100,000 white settlers took over a vast part of the Oklahoma plains.

59

HUNGRY AND HOPELESS

The Plains Indians had lost their territories. White Americans had given them reservations, but these were often on poor land, far from their old homes. Unable to grow or hunt for their own food, they depended on handouts from the government. On top of this, the summer of 1890 brought a new outbreak of deadly diseases such as measles and influenza.

Plains Indians were also losing their culture. On the reservations, the Sioux and Cheyennes were urged to give up their old religions. White **missionaries** and teachers lived among them and taught them about the Christian faith.

The lost children

Many white religious groups were devoted to the cause of making American Indians more "civilized." One group, called the Friends of the Indian, believed education in the style of the whites would speed this process. They took many American Indian children (some as young as five) away from their parents and put them in boarding schools further east. There they were forced to speak English, and they were punished if they spoke their own language. They had to wear pants, jackets, and dresses and give up their tribal way of life.[7]

A VISION

In 1888 a Paiute Indian in Nevada had a vision. In his vision, he was taken up into heaven, where God told him to teach his people to live in peace with the whites. He was also taught a special "ghost" dance. He was told that if all Indians performed the dance, evil would be swept away, and there would be a new age of love and plenty.

The Paiute's name was Wovoka. He began preaching the message of his vision and encouraging people to take part in the Ghost Dance. The new religion spread quickly. It clearly had echoes of the Christian faith, and soon Wovoka was calling himself "the Messiah," meaning he was a savior sent by God.[8]

During the Ghost Dance, Sioux dancers dressed in sacred "ghost" shirts, joined hands, and moved in a circle.

GHOST DANCE

The Sioux heard about the Ghost Dance in late 1890. In their desperate state, they saw the religion as an answer to their problems. If evil were swept away, that meant the white men would disappear as well. In a new land of plenty, the buffalo herds would return. Dead warriors would come back to life.

Huge numbers of Sioux and other American Indians began performing the Ghost Dance throughout the reservations. Some wore white "ghost" shirts, which they believed no bullet could pierce. Government agents were alarmed. They saw the dance as a sign of defiance and rebellion. Extra troops arrived in case of trouble.

One of the main centers of the Ghost Dance was Sitting Bull's village at Standing Rock. Early on the morning of December 15, 1890, a force of officers came to arrest Sitting Bull. They were all Lakota Indians who had joined the police.

A large crowd of angry Sioux gathered to watch. As their leader was being led away, one of them fired at the police. Immediately, an officer shot Sitting Bull through the head. The last of the great Plains Indian leaders fell dead.[9]

THE LAST DAYS

The Plains Indian Wars were nearly over. There was no revenge for the killing of Sitting Bull. His followers went to take refuge with another great Sioux chief, Red Cloud. Others were frightened by the violence and the growing troop numbers, and so they fled southward. One of the biggest of these groups was led by a chief named Big Foot.

THE WOUNDED KNEE MASSACRE

Troops of the 7th Cavalry caught up with Big Foot in South Dakota on December 28, 1890. The refugees were cold and hungry, and the chief himself was very sick. He surrendered, and the troops escorted the band to a camp at Wounded Knee Creek. The camp, which contained about 340 Sioux, was surrounded by a guard of 470 soldiers. Besides rifles, they had four Hotchkiss guns, which fired explosive shells.[10]

BIOGRAPHY

James W. Forsyth 1835–1906

BORN: Maumee, Ohio

ROLE: Commander of the 7th Cavalry at Wounded Knee

James W. Forsyth became a U.S. Army officer in 1856. In his long career, he took part in the Civil War and many campaigns during the Plains Indian Wars. He was appointed colonel of the 7th Cavalry in 1886. Many people accused Forsyth of deliberately planning to massacre Big Foot's party. All the same, the horror of Wounded Knee did not harm his career. He went on to become a major general, which is one of the highest ranks in the U.S. Army.

The next morning, soldiers went into the Sioux camp to search for weapons. The Sioux were scared and angry. Then there was an argument and a shot rang out. Immediately, the troops around the camp opened fire with their rifles and the Hotchkiss guns. "We tried to run but they shot us like we were a buffalo," said a Sioux girl who survived.[11]

In less than half an hour, as many as 250 Sioux were killed, and many others lay wounded. Most of the dead were women and children. About 25 soldiers were also killed, many by stray shots from their own side. A blizzard of snow covered the camp soon afterward, so the bodies could not be recovered until three days later. The Sioux corpses were buried in a long mass grave.[12]

The dead Sioux at Wounded Knee were left in the snow for three days before being buried in a mass grave.

THE END OF THE GHOST DANCE

After the Wounded Knee Massacre, some Plains Indians tried to get revenge. They burned U.S. government buildings and attacked wagon trains. But they had lost their fighting spirit. Now they knew that the Ghost Dance had failed, and that they could not defeat the white invaders. On January 16, 1891, the last group of hostile Sioux surrendered near Pine Ridge, South Dakota.

BLACK ELK, MEDICINE MAN

Black Elk was born in the Powder River Valley, in present-day Montana and Wyoming, in 1863. His family belonged to the Oglala band of the Lakota Sioux people. At the age of five, Black Elk began having visions. In one, a wild bird talked to him. In another, he rode on storm clouds and spoke with spirits in the sky who ruled the world. He realized he had the special gifts that could make him a Sioux medicine, or holy, man.[13] Medicine men were healers, and they could pray to the spirit world for help.

WITNESS TO WAR

During his long life, Black Elk was an eyewitness to two of the key moments in the Plains Indian Wars:

- In 1876, at about the age of 12, he took part in the Battle of the Little Bighorn. He killed and scalped several soldiers. From one dead body he took a watch, which he hung around his neck. He records one of the songs his people made up after the battle about the death of "Long Hair" (Custer).

> Long Hair, guns I had none.
> You brought me many. I thank you!
> You make me laugh!
> Long Hair, where he lies nobody knows.[14]

- In 1890 Black Elk was also present at the Wounded Knee Massacre. He heard the shooting and gathered men to attack the soldiers, but was driven off. As they rode, the Sioux sang:

> A thunder being nation I am, I have said.
> A thunder being nation I am, I have said.
> You shall live; you shall live; you shall live.[15]

BLACK ELK SPEAKS

Many years later, Black Elk recorded his life story in a famous book called *Black Elk Speaks*, which was published in 1932. A white writer named John Neihardt set his words down. Besides Black Elk's experiences and visions, the book described many Oglala religious rituals. *Black Elk Speaks* has become one of the most famous of all American Indian biographies.

▷ The Lakota medicine man Black Elk was a witness at the Battle of Little Bighorn and at Wounded Knee.

Death of a dream

Black Elk lived to be well over 80 years old. But he never forgot Wounded Knee. He said:

I did not know then how much was ended. When I look back now from this high hill of my old age, I can still see the butchered women and children lying heaped and scattered all along the crooked gulch. And I can see that something else also died there in the bloody mud, and was buried in the blizzard. A people's dream died there. It was a beautiful dream.[16]

WHAT HAVE WE LEARNED?

The Plains Indian Wars were very one-sided. American Indians won a few small battles, but in the end they lost the wars. When the wars ended in 1890, there were more than 17 million white people living west of the Mississippi River.[1] The number of American Indians in the whole United States at that time was fewer than 250,000. There was no realistic way they could have won.

RIGHTS AND WRONGS

The wars against the American Indians are still a sensitive subject today. Many people believe the white settlers' treatment of the Indians was shameful and amounted to **genocide**. Others think the defeat of the Indians was necessary in order to create one of the world's greatest nations. There are many arguments on both sides.

Here are some topics to discuss and think about:
- *The wars destroyed a unique way of life.*
  The cultures of the Plains Indians was unlike anything else in the world. Once the Plains were settled and the buffalo were wiped out, many aspects of these cultures disappeared.
- *North America provided homes for millions of people.*
  During the 19th century, the population of Europe and the eastern United States grew very fast. North America seemed like a rich and empty land waiting to be filled.
- *The Indians were cheated out of land that belonged to them.*
  White U.S. government representatives tricked the tribes into giving up their territories, and they broke solemn treaties. Should today's American Indians receive **compensation**?
- *The U.S. government could not please both pioneers and American Indians.*
  The government had to resolve the problems in the most practical way. What was the real impact of the idea of Manifest Destiny?

PLAINS INDIANS TODAY

In 1890 the Plains Indians were defeated, and they lacked the necessities for survival. Over a century later, most still live on reservations. These are often lacking in farmland and other resources. Many live in remote locations and lack good schools and medical services. American Indians are more likely than other Americans to be poor and unemployed.

But in recent years, American Indians have fought more actively for their **civil rights**. The American Indian Movement encourages Indians to take pride in their past and claim compensation for their treatment during the Plains Indian Wars. Its most famous action was the 1973 seizing of Wounded Knee, the site of the 1890 massacre. Protestors demanded a government review of the many treaties it had broken.[2]

In 2009 President Barack Obama signed a law that included an official apology to all American Indians. The statement stated it was "on behalf of the people of the United States to all Native Peoples for the many instances of violence, maltreatment, and neglect inflicted on Native Peoples by citizens of the United States."[3]

But there is still much social unrest today among American Indians. Many find it hard to maintain their cultural identity in a world where they are pushed to the side and disadvantaged. The tragedy of their treatment during the Plains Indian Wars still causes pain and anger today.

However, there are many American Indians who still maintain cultural traditions and rituals. They work to educate their descendants about their rich history and carry on the past.

TIMELINE

c. 1700   Plains Indians get their first horses, probably from Spanish people in Central America.

1776   After winning the Revolutionary War against Great Britain, the United States declares itself to be an independent country.

1803   In an event known as the Louisiana Purchase, the U.S. government buys the huge territory west of the Mississippi River from the French.

1830   As part of the Indian Removal Act, Eastern Indian tribes are forced to move to lands west of the Mississippi River, in present-day Oklahoma, to allow white settlement on their territory.

1838   Cherokee people are forced to move from Georgia to a new reservation in present-day Oklahoma, in a journey that comes to be known as the Trail of Tears, since many would die on the way.

1842   The first wagon train passes along the Oregon Trail.

1848   Gold is discovered in California. As a result, the traffic of settlers increases across Indian Territory.

1851   The first treaty with the Plains Indians is agreed upon at Fort Laramie, in what is now eastern Wyoming.

1854   U.S. troops are killed by American Indians near Fort Laramie, an event known as the Grattan Massacre.

1855   In response to the Grattan Massacre, the U.S. Army leads a revenge massacre in present-day Nebraska, known as the Battle of Ash Hollow or the Battle of Bluewater Creek.

1862   Little Crow leads a Sioux uprising in Minnesota.

1864   On November 29, in present-day Colorado, U.S. troops kill at least 160 Cheyennes, in an event known as the Sand Creek Massacre.

1865   In October, Cheyenne and Arapaho leaders sign the Treaty of Little Arkansas.

1866–68   The war known as Red Cloud's War is waged.

1866, July–August   U.S. forces establish three forts on the Bozeman Trail.

December 21   Sioux ambush and kill 80 soldiers near Fort Phil Kearny, in present-day Wyoming, in an event known as the Fetterman Massacre.

1867 August 2	Thirty-two U.S. soldiers from Fort Phil Kearny are attacked by about 1,000 Sioux, but manage to only lose three soldiers, in an event known as the Wagon Box Fight.
October	Most Southern Plains Indian tribes sign the Medicine Lodge Treaty, in which they agree to give up their tribal lands and move to smaller reservations in present-day Oklahoma.
1868 November 6	Red Cloud agrees to peace at Fort Laramie.
November 27	Custer massacres Cheyenne on the Washita River, in present-day Oklahoma.
1869	On May 10, a joining of the Union Pacific and Central Pacific railroads creates a railroad link across North America.
1870	In January, U.S. soldiers massacre 170 Blackfoot Indians in present-day Montana.
1871	The Indian Appropriations Act rules that American Indians are a single independent nation.
1874–75	The Red River War wages in the Texas Panhandle.
1874 June	Comanche and Kiowa attack white settlers in Adobe Walls, Texas.
July	Custer leads a white expedition into the Black Hills and finds gold: prospectors pour into the area.
1875	The U.S. government demands that the Plains Indians sell the Black Hills.
1876 May	A massive U.S. Army expedition begins to the Black Hills.
June 17	General Crook's column is attacked near Rosebud Creek, in present-day Montana.
June 25–26	Custer's forces are wiped out at the Little Bighorn.
August	The U.S. government orders the Sioux to leave the Black Hills.
November	The U.S. Army drives Plains Indians from the Black Hills.
1877 May	Sitting Bull crosses the border into Canada.
June–October	The Nez Percé flee the Wallowa Valley in Oregon, under Chief Joseph.
September 5	Crazy Horse dies.
1878	In September, the Cheyenne flee.
1881	In July, Sitting Bull returns from Canada to the United States.
1883	The last Sioux buffalo hunting expeditions take place.
1887	On February 8, the Dawes Act splits up American Indian reservations.
1889	On April 22, the first "land rush" into the Oklahoma Territory begins.
1890 October 9	News of the Ghost Dance religion reaches the Sioux reservation.
December 15	Sitting Bull is killed.
December 29	Big Foot's band is massacred by U.S. soldiers at Wounded Knee, in South Dakota.

GLOSSARY

ally close associate or supporter of another person or group

band (of Plains Indians) close-knit group of families, often related

brothel place where men pay to have sex with women

carcass dead body of an animal or person

cavalry troops who travel and fight on horseback

cholera very infectious and deadly disease, often caused by polluted water

civil rights the rights belonging to a person who is a citizen of a country or member of the community

civil war war between two parties in a single country

civilian anyone who is not a member of the armed forces

civilized taken out of a primitive state and made to conform to the culture of a developed society

column (battle) long formation of soldiers or vehicles

compensation payment to make amends for mistreatment or damage

corral enclosed area used for keeping animals in one place

culture customs, behavior, and beliefs of a particular race or nation of people

expedition journey by a group of people with a definite objective

exterminate complete wiping out, or killing, of something

frontier undeveloped land beyond a settled area

fur trapper someone who catches and kills animals (such as beavers) for their valuable fur

game wild animals hunted for food

genocide the wiping out of an entire race of people

hide the skin of an animal

homesteader someone who settles and farms a piece of land

Indian Territory the area of the United States set aside in 1834 as a homeland for groups of American Indians

livestock animals raised on farms for food or the materials they provide, such as cows or sheep

malaria infectious disease often spread by the bite of a mosquito

Manifest Destiny 19th-century doctrine which claimed that the United States had a moral right to expand over the continent of North America

massacre a savage killing of large numbers of people

missionary someone who works among nonbelievers to spread the message of his or her own religion

nation a people who share common customs, origins, history, and homeland

nomad someone who does not live in a permanent home, but rather moves around in search of food

oxen male cattle used to pull wagons and plows

pioneer person who travels to settle in wild or unknown country

prairie large area of flat grassland in North America

prairie chicken kind of bird of the grouse family found on the prairies

prospector person who searches for deposits of precious metals, such as gold

reservation area of land set aside for a special purpose (such as a new homeland for American Indians)

ritual special way of performing a religious ceremony

sacred connected with the worship of a god or other religious figure

scalp to cut off the hair and skin from the top of a victim's head

sinew tendon (the tough material that connects a muscle with a bone)

smallpox infectious disease that causes pimples and blisters

stockade barrier made of posts driven into the ground

surveyor someone who inspects land in advance of a building project and measures levels and distances

telegraph communications system that sends messages by electric impulses using Morse code

treaty signed agreement between two states or sides

tribe group of people with common ancestors living together under a chief

uncivilized not behaving or living in a way that conforms to the customs of a society that sees itself as civilized

vision dream, usually with some supernatural meaning

NOTES ON SOURCES

Peoples of the Plains (pages 4–9)
1. Ralph K. Andrist, *The Long Death: The Last Days of the Plains Indians* (New York: Collier Books, 1964), 354.
2. Andrist, *The Long Death*, 4.
3. Robert H. Lowie, *Indians of the Plains* (New York: McGraw Hill, 1954), 10.
4. Lowie, *Indians of the Plains*, 30.
5. Lowie, *Indians of the Plains*, 30.
6. *Ibid.*, 32.
7. Luther Standing Bear, *My People the Sioux* (Lincoln, NE: Bison Books, 1975), 14.
8. T. C. McLuhan, comp., *Touch the Earth: A Self-Portrait of Indian Existence* (London: Sphere Books, 1973), 64.
9. Alvin M. Josephy, *The Indian Heritage of America* (London: Penguin Books, 1975), 124.
10. Josephy, *The Indian Heritage of America*, 325.

Heading West (pages 10–15)
1. Andrist, *The Long Death*, 10.
2. *Ibid.*
3. Trevor B. McCrisken, *Exceptionalism: Manifest Destiny*, vol. 2 (New York: Scribner's, 2002), 68.
4. Dee Brown, *The American West* (New York: Scribner's, 1996), 32.
5. Dee Brown, *Wondrous Times on the Frontier* (London: Arrow Books, 1994), 17.
6. David Lavender, *The Penguin Book of the American West* (London: Penguin Books, 1989), 222.
7. Brown, *The American West*, 32.
8. Geoffrey C. Ward, *The West: An Illustrated History* (London: Weidenfeld & Nicolson, 1996), 154.
9. http://www.nps.gov/history/history/online_books/soldier/sitec9.htm
10. Andrist, *The Long Death*, 67.

The Plains Indian Wars Begin (pages 16–21)
1. Taylor and Sturtevant, *The Native Americans*, 146.
2. Andrist, *The Long Death*, 89.
3. Brad D. Lookingbill, "Black Kettle (ca. 1812–1868)," Oklahoma Historical Society's Encyclopedia of Oklahoma History and Culture, http://digital.library.okstate.edu/encyclopedia/entries/B/BL003.html.
4. *Ibid.*, 91.
5. Dee Brown, *Bury My Heart at Wounded Knee* (New York: Holt), 59.
6. Ward, *The West*, 204.
7. Ward, *The West*, 204.
8. Andrist, *The Long Death*, 94.
9. Josephy, *The Indian Heritage of America*, 339.
10. Brown, *Bury My Heart at Wounded Knee*, 79.

Red Cloud's War (pages 22–31)
1. Andrist, *The Long Death*, 101.
2. Andrist, *The Long Death*, 103.
3. PBS, "Red Cloud," *New Perspectives on the West*, http://www.pbs.org/weta/thewest/people/i_r/redcloud.htm.
4. Andrist, *The Long Death*, 104.
5. Ward, *The West*, 230.
6. Andrist, *The Long Death*, 108.
7. W. L. Holloway, ed., *Wild Life on the Plains and Horrors of Indian Warfare* (Whitefish, MT: Kessinger Publishing Company, 2006), 120.
8. Jerry Keenan, *The Wagon Box Fight* (Conshohocken, PA: Savas Publishing, 2000), 31.
9. *Ibid.*, 32.
10. *Ibid.*, 19.
11. Andrist, *The Long Death*, 131.
12. Andrist, *The Long Death*, 94.
13. Brown, *Bury My Heart at Wounded Knee*, 116.
14. *Ibid.*, 117.

15. Brown, *Bury My Heart at Wounded Knee*, 147.
16. *Ibid.*, 148.
17. *Ibid.*, 151.

Death on the Central Plains (pages 32–37)
1. Ward, *The West*, 254.
2. Ward, *The West*, 221.
3. *Ibid.*, 220–22.
4. Brown, *Bury My Heart at Wounded Knee*, 136.
5. The Wild West, "Annie Oakley," http://www. thewildwest.org/cowboys/ wildwestlegendarywomen/196.
6. Brown, *The American West*, 164–75.
7. Brown, *Bury My Heart at Wounded Knee*, 137.
8. The White House, "Ulysses S. Grant," http://www.whitehouse.gov/about/ presidents/ulyssessgrant.
9. Andrist, *The Long Death*, 171.
10. American Indian Civics Project, "Chronological Historical Overview, 1871 to 1924: Allotment and Assimilation," http:// americanindiantah.com/history/ cron_1871_1934.html.

Vanishing Herds (pages 38–43)
1. Brown, *Bury My Heart at Wounded Knee*, 211.
2. Andrist, *The Long Death*, 180.
3. Ward, *The West*, 263.
4. http://www.archives.gov/education/ lessons/homestead-act/
5. Taylor and Sturtevant, *The Native Americans*, 127.
6. Lowie, *Indians of the Plains*, 25.
7. *Ibid.*, 73.
8. Raymond De Maillie and Douglas R. Parks, eds., *Sioux Indian Religion: Tradition and Innovation* (Norman: University of Oklahoma Press, 1987), 32.
9. Texas State Library and Archives Commission, "Satanta," http://www. tsl.state.tx.us/treasures/indians/ satanta.html.
10. Andrist, *The Long Death*, 195.

11. Texas Beyond History, "Red River War," http://www. texasbeyondhistory.net/redriver/ index.html.

The Black Hills (pages 44–51)
1. Brown, *Bury My Heart at Wounded Knee*, 220.
2. Ward, *The West*, 293.
3. *Ibid.*, 295.
4. McLuhan, *Touch the Earth*, 90.
5. Brown, *Bury My Heart at Wounded Knee*, 217.
6. *Ibid.*, 225.
7. PBS, "Sitting Bull," *New Perspectives on the West*, http://www.pbs.org/weta/ thewest/people/s_z/sittingbull.htm.
8. Larry McMurtry, *Crazy Horse* (London: Weidenfeld & Nicolson, 1999), 13.
9. PBS, "Crazy Horse," *New Perspectives on the West*, http://www.pbs.org/weta/ thewest/people/a_c/crazyhorse.htm.
10. PBS, "Crazy Horse," *History Detectives*, http://www.pbs.org/opb/ historydetectives/investigations/705_ crazyhorse.html.
11. Evan S. Connell, *Son of the Morning Star: General Custer and the Battle of the Little Bighorn* (London: Pavilion Books, 1985), 67.
12. PBS, "George Crook," *New Perspectives on the West*, http://www. pbs.org/weta/thewest/people/a_c/ crook.htm.
13. Andrist, *The Long Death*, 265.
14. Connell, *Son of the Morning Star*, 259.
15. Ward, *The West*, 299.
16. PBS, "George Armstrong Custer," *New Perspectives on the West*, http:// www.pbs.org/weta/thewest/people/ a_c/custer.htm.
17. Connell, *Son of the Morning Star*, 103.
18. Connell, *Son of the Morning Star*, 105.
19. Andrist, *The Long Death*, 276.

Lost Homelands (pages 52–57)

1. Brown, *Bury My Heart at Wounded Knee*, 238.
2. PBS, "Chief Joseph," *New Perspectives on the West*, http://www.pbs.org/weta/thewest/people/a_c/chiefjoseph.htm.
3. McLuhan, *Touch the Earth*, 120.
4. Ward, *The West*, 280.
5. *Ibid.*, 375.
6. American Studies at the University of Virginia, "Buffalo Bill's Wild West Show: The Cast," http://xroads.virginia.edu/~hyper/hns/buffalobill/billcast.html.
7. Andrist, *The Long Death*, 333.
8. Brown, *The American West*, 245.
9. Ward, *The West*, 351.
10. Andrist, *The Long Death*, 334.

Land Rush (pages 58–65)

1. Kerry C. Kelly, "Teaching with Documents: Maps of Indian Territory, the Dawes Act, and Will Rogers' Enrollment Case File," National Archives, http://www.archives.gov/education/lessons/fed-indian-policy/.
2. Nebraska Studies, "The Dawes Act: 1887," http://www.nebraskastudies.org/0600/frameset_reset.html?http://www.nebraskastudies.org/0600/stories/0601_0200.html.
3. Lavender, *The Penguin Book of the American West*, 427.
4. Brown, *Bury My Heart at Wounded Knee*, 338.
5. Ward, *The West*, 390.
6. *Ibid.*, 340.
7. Ward, *The West*, 360.
8. Ghost Dance, "Ghost Dance of 1890," http://www.ghostdance.us/history/history-ghostdancewikipedia.html.
9. Andrist, *The Long Death*, 345.
10. Andrist, *The Long Death*, 348.
11. James H. McGregor, The Wounded Knee Massacre from the Viewpoint of the Survivors (Baltimore: Wirth Bros., 1940), 111.
12. Ward, *The West*, 401.
13. Black Elk and John Neihardt, *Black Elk Speaks: Being the Life Story of a Holy Man of the Oglala Sioux* (New York: William Morrow and Company, 1932), chap. 3.
14. *Ibid.*, chap. 7.
15. *Ibid.*, chap. 24.
16. *Ibid.*, chap. 25.

What Have We Learned? (pages 66–67)

1. Ward, *The West*, 394.
2. Laura Waterman Wittstock and Elaine J. Salinas, "A Brief History of the American Indian Movement," American Indian Movement, http://www.aimovement.org/ggc/history.html.
3. John D. McKinnon, "U.S. Offers an Official Apology to Native Americans," *Wall Street Journal*, December 22, 2009, http://blogs.wsj.com/washwire/2009/12/22/us-offers-an-official-apology-to-native-americans/.

BIBLIOGRAPHY

BOOKS

Andrist, Ralph K. *The Long Death: The Last Days of the Plains Indians*. New York: Collier Books, 1993.

Brown, Dee. *The American West*. New York: Scribner's, 1996.

Brown, Dee. *Bury My Heart at Wounded Knee: An Indian History of the American West*. New York: Sterling Publications, 2009.

Brown, Dee. *Wondrous Times on the Frontier*. Little Rock, AR: August House Publishers, 1991.

Connell, Evan S. *Son of the Morning Star: General Custer and the Battle of the Little Bighorn*. San Francisco: North Point Press, 1984.

Josephy, Alvin M. *The Indian Heritage of America*. Boston: Houghton Mifflin, 1991.

Lavender, David. *The Penguin Book of the American West*. London: Penguin Press, 1989.

Lowie, Robert H. *Indians of the Plains*. Lincoln, NE: University of Nebraska Press, 1985.

McLuhan, T. C., comp. *Touch the Earth: A Self-Portrait of Indian Existence*. New York: Promontory Press, 1993.

McMurtry, Larry. *Crazy Horse*. New York: Penguin Press, 2006.

Taylor, Colin F., and William C. Sturtevant. *The Native Americans: The Indigenous People of North America*. San Diego: Thunder Bay Press, 1999.

Ward, Geoffrey C. *The West: An Illustrated History*. Boston: Little, Brown, 1996.

FIND OUT MORE

The story of the Plains Indians and the pioneers of the United States is a thrilling one. There is much more to find out about this subject, and there are plenty of sources to try. Here are some suggestions for getting to know more about the topic.

BOOKS

Brook, Henry. *The Wild West (Usborne True Stories)*. Tulsa, Okla.: EDC, 2008.

Hatt, Christine. *The American West (Questioning History)*. North Mankato, Minn.: Smart Apple Media, 2005.

McPherson, James M. *Into the West: From Reconstruction to the Final Days of the American Frontier*. New York: Atheneum, 2006.

Morley, Jacqueline. *How Would You Survive in the American West?* New York: Franklin Watts, 2005.

Murdoch, David Hamilton. *North American Indian (DK Eyewitness)*. New York: Dorling Kindersley, 2005.

Santella, Andrew. *Plains Indians (First Nations of North America)*. Chicago: Heinemann Library, 2012.

Steele, Christy. *Pioneer Life in the American West*. Milwaukee: World Almanac Library, 2005.

WEBSITES

www.indians.org/articles/american-indians.html
This website provides a detailed history of all American Indian peoples.

www.aimovement.org
This official American Indian Movement website is full of information about American Indian history, written from the perspective of American Indians. You can also learn about what is going on in their culture today.

www.pbs.org/wgbh/amex/weshallremain/
This PBS multimedia experience explores the role of American Indians in U.S. history.

DVDS

There are hundreds of Hollywood movies about the Plains Wars. Many of these are romantic stories that give a misleading picture of what actually happened. But some show something close to the truth. There are also many documentaries that show the reality of what American Indians went through. The following is a selection of movies and documentaries that sympathize with American Indians and give a realistic picture of their daily lives, attitudes, and customs.

Cheyenne Autumn (Burbank, Calif.: Warner Home Video, 2011; originally released 1964).
This film addresses the tragedy of the flight of the Cheyenne from Oklahoma in 1878 and their treatment at the hands of white soldiers and civilians.

Fort Apache (Burbank, Calif.: Warner Brothers Home Video, 2006; originally released 1948).
John Wayne plays an arrogant Indian-hating officer in this study of relations between the two races.

Little Big Man (Hollywood, Calif.: Paramount Home Entertainment, 2003; originally released 1970).
This is an entertaining account of a white child raised by the Cheyenne. It gives a convincing picture of the daily life of American Indians.

Native American Legends (Manhattan, NY: A&E Home Video, 2008).
Learn about the amazing accomplishments of legendary American Indians during conflicts.

The Searchers (Burbank, Calif.: Warner Home Video, 1997; originally released 1956).
This tells the story of the hunt for a little girl kidnapped by Comanche. It examines the hatred felt by many white Americans for American Indians.

We Shall Remain (Arlington, VA: PBS Home Video, 2009).
This documentary tells about some of the most important moments in history of the United States from the American Indian perspective.

INDEX